PRAISE FOR *FEARLESS FEEDBACK*

"So much in this book resonates with me. Brimming with nuggets of purposeful insight, these master coaches deliver a masterful feedback guidebook for both leaders and coaches."

—**Richard Leider, international best-selling author of**
The Power of Purpose, Repacking Your Bags, **and** *Life Reimagined*

"What an outstanding book you have written and what an important contribution to the field of coaching. The seven-step model is crystal clear, the cases are strong illustrations, and the templates will be sought after! Bravo to each and every one of you."

—**Dr. Pamela D. McLean, CEO The Hudson Institute of Santa Barbara,**
Author of *The Completely Revised Handbook of Coaching*

"Everyone understands in theory that leaders should get feedback from the key people around them. It sounds so simple; the coach just does a few interviews and writes a report, job done! In practice it needs careful preparation from coach and client, and exquisite ability to listen and to debrief in a way that the client can hear. This book does all of this—and more. It is clear, well written, and has the authentic feel of real life. Every executive coach should read it."

—**Jenny Rogers, Master Executive Coach, Coach Instructor, and author of**
Coaching Skills: The Definitive Guide to Being a Coach,
and *Coaching with Personality Type*

"Courageously developing others with caring and direct feedback is both challenging and critical in our hyperactive, driven world. *Fearless*

Feedback gives you the comprehensive and pragmatic tools needed to navigate leadership roles with purpose, clarity, and conviction. A great leadership guide for us all!"

—**Kevin Cashman, Global Leader, CEO & Exec Development at Korn Ferry**
Best-selling author of *Leadership from the Inside Out* and *Pause Point*

"This book is a real contribution to a part of the coaching process often used, sometimes botched, but in general underutilized for lack of deliberation about the steps, the pitfalls, and the opportunities. As a veteran in the field I found it useful and it made me think anew, and I wish I'd had access to it when I started coaching."

—**John Schuster, Executive Coach, Founder Schuster-Kane Alliance,**
Author of *Answering Your Call* and *The Power of Your Past*

"Clear, honest, and humane feedback is one of the most important tools we have to improve performance and develop leadership. But guess what? We're human, and feedback is hard—both for the giver as well as the receiver. Feedback is rarely easy, and the last thing we want to do is make things worse. The real question is: What are we going to do about this?

"Into this void step the authors of the book *Fearless Feedback*. The master coaches who have written this book lay out a step-by-step guide to gathering, delivering, and working with feedback. They show you how to do it right. The book is specific and actionable, and is especially noteworthy for the ongoing use of 'do this, not that' examples, as well as the depictions of the unverbalized conversations that are going on underneath actual feedback conversations. Whether you are a leader, a coach, or just a conscious human being, if you are serious about mastering feedback, this book is for you!"

—**Michael Melcher, Executive Coach and Partner, Next Step Partners**
Author of *The Creative Lawyer: A Practical Guide to Authentic Professional Satisfaction*

"A timely and urgently needed book for leadership coaches. It lays bare the essential practices for gathering and delivering meaningful stakeholder feedback to foster deep positive change within the system of relationships where the leader operates."

—**Redia Anderson, PCC, Executive Coach,**
Chief Diversity & Inclusion Officer, BP (retired)
Author of *Trailblazers: How Top Business Leaders Are Accelerating Results*

"A Must-Read!! Every leadership and executive coach offering stakeholder feedback interviews and insight debriefs, no matter what level of experience, will benefit from this. The transmitter metaphor offering signal strength and alignment to goal is brilliant! The sample coaching vignettes not only bring the guidebook tools to life, they make it real!"

—**Ann E. Boyum, PCC, CALC and Certified Supervision Coach**

"The corporate landscape is littered with wounded relationships, injured by well-meaning but poorly implemented multi-rater feedback initiatives. This competent and compassionate team of coaches has co-authored a book that will expand the consciousness of both the givers and receivers of feedback. The realistic, well-articulated vignettes help practitioners recognize and prepare for the psychological impact of stakeholder feedback: the reactions, projections, and emotions that accompany even the best processes. Because feedback is as much about the giver as the receiver, *Fearless Feedback* aims to help create a field of trust from which change, even healing, can happen."

—**Lynn Schoener, Executive and Team Coach**
Founder, Coaching Creative Change

"Senior leaders often operate to their detriment without much feedback from stakeholders. This is a practical guide developed by a team of master coaches for how a coach can work effectively with a senior leader to close the feedback gap. It is essential reading for anyone coaching a senior leader."

—Lyndon Rego, Executive Director,
Center for Entrepreneurial Leadership, African Leadership Academy

"How many Master Coaches does it take to write a book that provides a comprehensive framework and illustration of the end-to-end process of collecting and delivering feedback to leaders? Seven, evidently! 360-degree feedback is (or should be) a staple in every coach's tool kit. But until reading this book, I'd never seen such a clear step-by-step process of how to do it or a complete examination of all of the factors to consider. And that's not even what I love most about it.

"This book fully explores the critical importance of attuning and attending to the emotional experience of the leader being coached throughout the feedback process. The feedback process can be a minefield for any coach who doesn't mindfully attend to the internal experience of their coachee. The authors have adroitly addressed specifically how to work with the emotions of leaders to avoid the hidden emotional land mines that can be obstacles to the feedback process.

"If you are gathering feedback for your leaders (and if you aren't, you probably want to be), buy this book! It'll walk you through the entire process, providing tips and techniques for how to make it all work to the leader's benefit—and avoid the mines!"

—Alison Whitmire
President, EQ Learning In Action

"Changing behavior is a key outcome in any coaching relationship. Who would know if someone changed as a result of your coaching? Stakeholders. Thus, active engagement of stakeholders, and accurate delivery of their suggestions, can make or break the engagement. How to access and translate stakeholder viewpoints is well described and documented with excellent examples throughout this book. I can't imagine anyone in the coaching profession who would not grow as a result of incorporating these ideas.

"I also love that these ideas are the collective thoughts of a team. I can imagine the rich conversations they must have had in bringing their experiences together. Readers are treated with multiple but cohesive perspectives. It's rare that we see a book written by a team of authors. The diversity of thought that went into their collective thinking makes their suggestions incredibly thorough."

—Dr. Beverly Kaye, Founder Career Systems International,
Author of *Love 'Em or Lose 'Em, Help Them Grow or Watch Them Go,*
and *Learn Like a Leader*

"This book educates you on how to be a great coach by coaching you. It is deliberate and challenging. If you find yourself reaching for ways to work with difficult clients, get to know Greta, the coach character in this book, and her client Richard. You will have a framework in your pocket that spells success! Key message—you can only take your client as deep as you, yourself, are able to go."

—Dr. Jacqueline Byrd, CEO of Creatrix,
Innovation Consultant and Executive Coach,
Author of *The Innovation Equation* and *Voice of the Innovator,*
Owner of the Creatrix Innovation Assessment and Process

"Whether you are a seasoned coach, just getting started, or working inside organizations, *Fearless Feedback* is the go-to guidebook for generating and delivering stakeholder feedback. *Fearless Feedback* provides an in-depth framework to help you get the most out of this important process, and navigate the emotions of all involved."

—**Dave Wondra, Past Chair International Coaching Federation (ICF),**
Executive Coach, President, Wondra Group

"What makes a great coach? Start with a great human, add strong coaching skills, spend countless hours in practice, reflect, adjust, learn. This book is an accelerator created for you by a team of fine human beings who are experienced coaches ever striving to be better. With generosity they give you this boost. Don't skim the personal insights in the preface. You'll enjoy the case study with Richard and Greta. The Framework is elegant and actionable. I am blessed to be in relationship with these fine people, and this guidebook is a great tool. Enjoy!"

—**Sandy Smith, Master Credentialed Executive Coach,**
Hudson Institute Leadership Team, Master Coach Program Faculty

FEARLESS FEEDBACK

A Guide for Coaching Leaders to See Themselves More Clearly and Galvanize Growth

REBECCA GLENN, PENNY HANDSCOMB, AMY KOSTERLITZ, KATHLEEN MARRON, KELLY ROSS, LORI SIEGWORTH, AND TIMOTHY SIGNORELLI

Limits of Liability and Disclaimer of Warranty:

The purpose of this book is to educate and entertain. While the authors and/or publisher have used best efforts in preparing this book, they make no representations regarding accuracy and completeness of ideas, examples, practices and experiments provided within, and specifically disclaim any implied warrants of merchantability or fitness for a particular purpose. The authors and/or publisher do not guarantee that anyone following these techniques, suggestions, tips, ideas, or strategies will become successful. The authors and/or publisher shall have neither liability nor responsibility to anyone with respect to any loss or damage caused, or alleged to be caused, directly or indirectly by the information contained in this book. Case examples are intentionally anonymized, and sometimes are composites, to more concisely convey particular learning points, and any resemblance to actual individuals is purely accidental. The authors and/or publisher shall not be liable for your misuse of this material. The contents are strictly for informational and educational purpose only. Further, readers should be aware that Internet websites listed in this work may have changed or disappeared between when this work was written and when it is read.

Printed and bound in the United States of America
ISBN: 978-0-578-40905-4
Library of Congress Control Number: 2018965372

DEDICATION

This book is humbly dedicated to the incredible faculty of The Hudson Institute 2016 Master Coach Program, Pam McLean, Sandy Smith, and Doug Silsbee. Your encouragement and "request" became the impetus for this work.

And to our loved ones, our deepest thanks for your patience and support throughout this creative process. We couldn't be where we are without you.

CONTENTS

CHAPTER SEVEN

Stakeholder Feedback Framework Step 6:

CHAPTER EIGHT

Stakeholder Feedback Framework Step 7:

APPENDIX

FOREWORD

By Dr. Pamela McLean

In the many years that I have trained master coaches and engaged in executive coaching myself, I have consistently observed the power and importance of the stakeholder feedback process in the work of leadership coaching. Without stakeholder input from the leader's system, the coach and leader are working in a vacuum, with inadequate input and perspectives relative to the leader's development. The work of gathering stakeholder input is both an art and a science with multiple challenges in the path. Leaders may be reluctant to engage in the process, stakeholders need to be reassured of confidentiality in order to ensure candidness, and coaches need to be adeptly skilled at managing the stakeholder conversations, compiling the feedback and presenting it to the leader (client) in a manner that allows the leader to hear it and land on what is most helpful in the coaching work going forward.

The collection of stakeholder input in leadership coaching is complex, as it requires a coach to interface with the systems their client is immersed in, and it often uncovers unexpected nuances along the way. To gain maximum value from this process, a coach cannot rely on a prepackaged one-size-fits-all template. Instead, a coach needs to cultivate the ability to work within the system, culling out interactions, patterns of behaviors, and systemic influences embedded in the culture.

This book makes a unique contribution to the field of leadership coaching, providing a comprehensive view of the complexities and dimensions of the stakeholder process by deftly outlining a seven-step pathway. From the first step of identifying stakeholders to the final step of building a development plan, this book takes an in-depth look at each segment, providing valuable case studies as well as templates and recommendations for a coach's consideration. Acknowledging the need for coaches to calibrate and adjust their approach in each unique situation, the authors also emphasize foundational competencies and capacities that need to be cultivated by the coach in order to successfully engage in this rigorous process—a well-established working alliance with the leader (coachee) and a thoroughly developed coaching presence.

In the past several years, I have devoted much of my work in the field of coaching to the concept of self-as-coach, the internal landscape of a coach requiring continual cultivation in order to engage in developmental coaching able to foster deep change. These master coaches embody the very best of the self-as-coach concept in this seven-step stakeholder process. Their framework begins by underlining the coach's need to build a working alliance and develop a trusting relationship through their use of self before engaging in the stakeholder process; they also highlight the necessity of full presence at each step in the process. Without these core qualities, this work would be significantly diminished.

I have had the opportunity to work with this remarkably talented group of master coach authors on many occasions over the years. First, when each participated in Hudson's yearlong coach certification program; and again in 2016 when all these authors participated in our five-month master coach program. Our master coach program at Hudson is created for coach practitioners with significant coaching experience who want to deepen their capacity as coaches. It is experientially focused, and a centerpiece of the learning is engaging in a real-time stakeholder experience in the roles of coach and client. This practice allows a coach to examine this process from all directions within the stakeholder system. One of the most powerful learnings that unfolds is a personal understanding of the courage and humility that is required to sit in the role of the client and receive stakeholder feedback, and the skill that is demanded of the coach to provide the feedback in a manner that allows the client to absorb it and use it in a way that serves them as a leader. At Hudson, we have been conducting master coach classes for several years, and in this particular course, I was struck by how deeply engaged this group of coaches was in culling out all the nuanced layers of learning possible in the stakeholder exercise.

I am honored that the master coach authors for this guidebook began their journey at Hudson and have fully forged their own path. I look forward to seeing the impact of this framework as it is adopted by coaches committed to the work of leadership coaching.

Dr. Pamela McLean

CEO, The Hudson Institute of Santa Barbara

Author, *The Completely Revised Handbook of Coaching: A Developmental Approach*

PREFACE

We began this journey as master coaches by asking one shared question: When feedback plays such an important role in boosting leaders' professional growth, why is it so hard to obtain candid and constructive feedback about a leader and deliver it well in the context of an executive coaching engagement?

We are colleagues who, together, have worked on answering this question. Now we want to share the important lessons we have learned with fellow leadership (or executive) coaches, leaders, and people they impact. In our own search for a better way to navigate feedback, we gained heightened awareness of the impact emotions have in the feedback process. This book is the culmination of many "aha" moments about what can make or break a good feedback process in a coaching engagement, and we offer it as a leaping-off point for others on a similar journey.

Our Purpose: Why Read This Guidebook?

Obtaining and delivering stakeholder feedback can be challenging because leaders often encounter unexpected emotional reactions—

their own and their stakeholders'. We realized that emotional reactions to feedback cannot be explored in-depth with a typical organizational "360" review process. It was clear to us that an off-the-shelf (often online) feedback tool, quantitatively scored and survey-based, cannot reveal an interview's nuances and details or provide the kind of individualized feedback tailored to meet the needs of different kinds of leaders.

While much has been written about coaching and delivering feedback, very little has been written on *how* to effectively conduct and leverage stakeholder feedback interviews in executive coaching engagements, and the best practices and templates for doing so.[1] Three themes emerged in our review of the literature:[2]

▶ There are many benefits for leaders to collecting and receiving feedback from a range of sources; feedback is critical for growth.

▶ Feedback can be difficult to hear; the feedback deliverer needs to be mindful of debriefing feedback in a way the recipient can hear it and act on it, despite emotional triggers.

▶ Execution of feedback matters, and many write about the pitfalls of poorly executed feedback collection and delivery.

There are also a number of resources written for organizations collecting feedback as part of performance evaluations. While we pulled the

---

1 The most specific mention of the role stakeholder interviews can play in executive coaching is contained in *The Completely Revised Handbook of Coaching: A Developmental Approach*, by Dr. Pam McLean (John Wiley & Sons, 2012). In this handbook, McLean provides a description of an ideal process, including suggested questions for the interview, and we drew upon that work in creating the framework presented in this guidebook.

2 To make sure what we intended to offer the coaching community was unique, we conducted a thorough review of the literature to see what had previously been written on these topics. One of our fellow master coaches, Leslie Goldenberg, contributed invaluably to the literature review, for which we are deeply grateful. We want to acknowledge her contributions. See the acknowledgments for more details on our support from Leslie and others.

lessons relevant from that work, it is not the focus of our book, which is focused on feedback in furtherance of the leader's own development.

We created this guidebook to address these challenges and gap in the literature. We created a model for collecting, structuring, and delivering stakeholder feedback that would be more in-depth, customized, and supportive of a leader's goals, while attending to emotional reactions. We built the Stakeholder Feedback Framework as a way to provide coaches with new perspectives, and leaders with constructive suggestions that would help them achieve their development goals.

Our Readers: Whom Did We Hope to Reach?

When we were considering who our ideal audience would be for this book, we realized that most of our readers were likely going to be fellow executive coaches (from the newly minted to the very seasoned). After we began creating the framework, we saw that there were also lessons there for leaders who desire to bring a coaching mindset to managing others and for boards who want to offer feedback to their CEOs. We also realized that this framework may provide valuable insights to HR professionals and others who want to expand their skills in gathering feedback as part of the coaching or managing of leaders.

In writing this guidebook, therefore, we focused primarily on questions such as how do we as executive leadership coaches gather feedback, deliver it, and use it to guide leaders to become the most effective leaders they can be?

If you are an executive leadership coach and identify with any of the following scenarios, many tools and tips in this book were created for you.

- ▶ Perhaps you're just starting out as an executive leadership coach and want to learn a framework and some best practices for how to conduct stakeholder interviews.
- ▶ Perhaps you've been coaching for decades and have conducted many 360 reviews of leaders but would like to learn an alternative to off-the-shelf (often online) quantitatively scored surveys focused on performance. You are looking for a new way to co-create with the leaders you coach a stakeholder feedback process tailored to the leaders' development goals.
- ▶ You are already conducting stakeholder interviews as part of coaching engagements. You realize they sometimes go well and other times not so well. You would like to gain insights about how to repeat your successes and avoid the pitfalls.
- ▶ You are curious about what role your emotions, as well as those of the leaders you coach and the stakeholders you interview, play in the process, and you wonder how you can increase your emotional intelligence to improve as a coach.

Our Story: Who Are We?

We are a group of master executive coaches who studied the role of stakeholder feedback in leadership coaching as part of the Hudson Institute of Coaching's Master Coach Program (MCP). This work strengthened our conviction that stakeholder feedback is an essential element of an effective leadership coaching engagement. It also provided us with an opportunity to experience first-hand the challenges and rewards of the feedback process, and to learn some lessons about best practices and pitfalls that we wanted to share with the coaching community.

Our MCP group (fondly known as the "MC-Peeps") brings a diverse perspective. Some of us are, or have been, internal coaches, well acquainted with the role feedback plays in organizations; others are external coaches who have provided coaching and gathered feedback for leaders in a wide variety of professions and industries, including education, financial services, healthcare, insurance, law, media and entertainment, oil and gas, professional services, technology, renewable energy, and not-for-profit organizations. We have had successful careers in other professions before being certified as coaches, and we focus our coaching on Executive Leaders. We each also have earned the International Coaching Federation ("ICF") certification of Professional Certified Coach (PCC) and the Master Coach credential with the Hudson Institute of Coaching. We are international with several decades of experience collectively, and serve leaders living and working in several countries.

Our interest in improving the feedback process motivated us to pool our collective experience and inspired us to realize we wanted to learn more. The seeds for envisioning what was possible were sown in the immersive stakeholder feedback process that was a part of our firsthand experiential learning in the Master Coach Program.

Our Inspiration: Immersive Master Coach Learning

In the Hudson Institute's Master Coach learning program, each master coach had the opportunity to play the three key roles in the process of gathering and delivering stakeholder feedback: (1) as the coach, (2) as a leader being coached, and (3) as a stakeholder providing feedback about the leader.

One aspect of this stakeholder research learning was to randomly assign each of us to play the roles of coach and leader. This randomness allowed us to feel the vulnerability that leaders may sometimes feel when they have been "assigned" a coach (rather than choosing one for themselves). It also reminded us that even when a leader selects their own coach (and isn't randomly assigned to one), vulnerability is still present. It became clear to us at a visceral level how critically important it is to create an emotionally safe environment in order for real learning to take place.

It turns out each of us was not just playing a role; we were also making the emotional and conceptual connections that would allow us to collaborate and form our author team. The lessons we share in this book are based on some of the most deeply felt experiences we had during the Master Coach Program.

The following are a few critical examples of what shaped our thinking for the Stakeholder Feedback Framework. Each individual story would later become a moment of group revelation. In each instance, one of us perceived something that was true for all of us.

▶ One of us assigned the role of a leader being coached experienced great angst over providing the names of real coaching clients to be interviewed by the coach assigned to her. What would that coach say in these interviews? What would her CEO clients think of the whole process? This anxiety could have led to friction between the coach and the leader being coached—friction over both the content of the questions and how the answers would be recorded. We learned the importance of having a trusting relationship firmly in place between the coach and the leader being coached before commencing stakeholder interviews.

▶ One of us had an experience where the assigned coach predetermined the entire stakeholder structure, questions, and approach without collaboration or input at all from the leader. As a result, there was a tendency for the leader to feel quite defensive and disempowered—as if she was not a collaborative partner with the coach. In short, we learned there needed to be a stronger working alliance built between the coach and the leader.

▶ One of us in the role of the leader co-created questions with her coach only to learn later that the coach had asked a number of additional questions which the leader did not feel were relevant to her. Later, the coach explained he had thought the questions being asked by other coaches were interesting and added them (without checking with the leader being coached). The lesson learned in this instance was the need to ensure alignment with the leader about the questions that will be asked and goals for the feedback, in advance of commencing the stakeholder interviews.

▶ One of us learned something unexpected while serving as a stakeholder for another coach. When it came time to answer specific questions and provide feedback, the coach serving as stakeholder became anxious and wondered if she had enough personal interactions with the coach to add value. She wanted to be helpful although she felt very uncertain. Would her feedback reflect an important learning for the coach? Until then, the coach serving as stakeholder had never focused on the fact that being a stakeholder can be an emotionally challenging role, even when you want to be very good at it.

▶ One of us in the role of a leader being coached felt hurt when their coach reported a stakeholder's use of a derogatory label, with no supporting behavioral examples. This led to the leader fixating on the negative comment, to the exclusion of any positive comments. This underscored the need for a coach to exercise discretion about whether to report opinions when there is no link to identified behaviors. Hindsight taught us that questions need to be asked in the stakeholder interview to elicit actionable behavioral observations (rather than just a stereotype which might reflect the bias of the stakeholder).

▶ One of us in the role of a leader experienced a feedback debrief in which they felt the need to try to address all the stakeholder comments, regardless of their magnitude or priority. This led to a lack of focus and a feeling of being overwhelmed. The coach masterfully refocused the leader's attention on the purpose of the feedback—to help the leader achieve their goals. The leader was then able to discern what aspects of the feedback they wanted to address. This artful coach demonstrated the importance of putting the feedback into perspective and reminding the leader that the feedback is in service to their developmental goals.

▶ One of us was assigned a coach and reached out to stakeholders to invite their feedback, anxious about what would be heard and intrigued about the learning opportunity. The assigned master coach was exceptional in how she guided the process and delivered the information gathered from the stakeholders. This coach made the experience fulfilling, energizing, and inspiring for the leader. We learned that feedback delivered well could be transformational for a leader.

Our individual learnings were illuminating and transformational. Each of us felt motivated to continue learning as a Master Executive Coach, and the experiences we shared with each other turned into a strong desire to share with an even broader community of coaches.

Our Framework: How Was It Created?

As we shared our stories with one another, we were struck by the powerful discoveries we each had as coach, leader, and stakeholder. This project provided us with a rich arena to experience the emotions, challenges, and opportunities of all three distinct roles. We also pooled our resources, identifying best practices and tools each of us had created over the years. We were determined to distill our learnings on how to effectively collect and apply stakeholder feedback as part of an executive coaching engagement.

We created a model of seven key steps in the stakeholder feedback process. This became our Stakeholder Feedback Framework. The framework is based on a solid foundation of two elements that permeate each step; this foundation ensures the trust and emotional safety needed to gather and receive feedback. Emotional safety is defined as the emotional state in a trusting relationship that allows the parties to be open and vulnerable without fear of repercussion.

We then wanted to share what we had learned with the Hudson executive coaching community in some form of live demonstration. We particularly wanted to give the audience for the live demo a way to visualize the powerful emotions impacting the effectiveness of a feedback process. Inspired by the Disney Pixar movie *Inside Out*, we created a live demonstration to show the interactions of a coach, a leader, and two sample stakeholders in feedback situations. In the demonstration, we enacted the roles of the participants and their emotions popping up behind the scenes (as reflected by emotion words on sticks raised over each speaker's head, with oral commentary, to show the audience the emotions bubbling under the surface for each person being interviewed or coached).When we performed in front of a live audience of approximately 250 executive coaches in 2017, we received comments about how compelling it was to see and hear the emotional undercurrents in coaching, particularly in a setting involving feedback.

Based on this positive encouragement, we fleshed out the framework and made it come to life with more coaching stories to illustrate the emotional backdrop of each step. This gave rise to the guidebook before you.

We are moved by our desire to deliver tremendous value to the leaders we coach, and we know you feel this too. We hope our guidebook will help you enhance your skills at gathering feedback, so that you may enjoy the enormous privilege of building a trusting relationship with leaders and their stakeholders. Along the way, we hope you have some fun reading our stories about the emotional highs and lows in the stakeholder feedback process.

INTRODUCTION

"Without good feedback mechanisms and without feed-
back given and received in ways that enable real learning
(rather than defensiveness), people (leaders) can't learn,
and the early and weak signals of coming change are lost."

—Jennifer Garvey Berger and Keith Johnston,
Simple Habits for Complex Times: Powerful Practices for Leaders

The metaphor of sending and receiving signals used in the above quotation captures the essence of the feedback experience that inspired the creation of our framework, the writing of this book, and the work of the stakeholder feedback process. Signals are not explicit communications. They are gestures, cues, and signs that often require a nuanced interpreter; they are sometimes imperceptible or difficult to decode. Leaders need tools to decipher the subtle signals of coming change and their own need to change. Stakeholders can be both signal interpreters and the living, breathing signals of impending and desired changes for a leader. At best, executive coaches can be the facilitators of accurate signal transmission and reception.

The premise of this guidebook is simple: stakeholder feedback in coaching is essential for helping leaders to understand what they signal to others and how others can serve as signals for changes in the leader's development path. Through coach-orchestrated stakeholder feedback, leaders gain insight into how their behavior is perceived, which helps them make desired improvements. The signaling metaphor is woven throughout this guidebook, to help illustrate the ways in which all participants can improve their ability to send and receive clear messages.

The leaders we coach often express the opinion that stakeholder feedback (when done well) is among the most valuable experiences they receive in the coaching process. We address stakeholder feedback in the context of leadership coaching engagements, and we breathe life into this context with vignettes focused on two fictional leaders—Sue and Richard—who must negotiate some of the vulnerabilities, hazards, and emotional signals we ourselves negotiated while immersed in the stakeholder feedback process.

Our goal is to assist coaches in eliciting candid, constructive feedback from key people in a leader's world, and to deliver the feedback artfully so the leader can make positive and sustainable behavior changes. This guidebook is designed to help coaches and leaders hear and decode the weak signals of change so that they become audible and clear. Before we dive into the tips, tools, and techniques, we want to define a few key terms and discuss some of the book's most valuable features for our readers.

Defining Feedback and Other Key Terms

As we mentioned in our preface, the story of our coming together as authors centers around feedback. Feedback means many things to many people; it is both desired and dreaded. In this book, we use the term "feedback" to mean requested information about a leader from those who work with them about what it is like interacting with that leader, with an aim toward equipping that leader to achieve their future goals. To borrow from Garvey Berger (2015, p. 72), we can say this information includes *data* (facts about the leader's behavior), *emotions and impressions* (feelings and assumptions on the part of the stakeholders), as well as the *impact* the leader has on others.

Since the Feedback Framework applies to coaches both external and internal to the organization, we refer to the person being coached as the *leader* (rather than client).[3] The leader's organization, if it is paying for the coaching, is the *sponsor* in the coaching process: the individual within that organization who will be the coach's contact is the *sponsoring party*, which can sometimes be the leader's supervisor, and sometimes is a representative from Human Resources, or the Chief Talent Officer (if the organization has one). The *stakeholders* are typically people chosen from the leader's professional organization or circles of influence who have an interest in or are impacted by the leader and have an opportunity to observe the leader in their role. Typically, stakeholders may include supervisors, peers, direct reports, and, in some cases, the organization's board members or leader's clients or customers.

What Can This Book Offer Readers?

Whether you are a beginner coach or seasoned master coach, an external coach who runs your own business, or an internal coach who

---

3 We use this more comprehensive term of "leader" in lieu of "client" or "coachee" (which are also terms some external coaches would use to refer to the leaders they coach).

is part of the organization of the leaders you coach, this guidebook can help you achieve a new level of comfort and mastery with the process of gathering and delivering feedback as part of a leadership coaching engagement. This process requires managing your emotions and being attuned to the emotions of others. Mastery involves learning new ways to excel at being you as a coach, playing to your strengths, being aware of your potential blind spots, and enhancing your emotional intelligence to create a rich and valuable experience for the leaders you coach.

This guidebook was created to give you the power to:

▶ Persuade the leaders you coach of the benefits of a co-created stakeholder feedback process that serves the leaders' development goals.

▶ Know more about the significant role that emotions play in gathering and delivering feedback to leaders and how to manage these emotions skillfully (your own as well as those of the leaders and their stakeholders).

▶ Apply a step-by-step framework that will make gathering feedback about the leaders you coach a positive experience for all involved, with tools to structure, conduct, and deliver stakeholder feedback interviews and client debriefs with ease.

▶ Take your coaching to the next level of mastery and use the stakeholder feedback process to build and enhance the trust and presence you need as a master coach.

▶ Anticipate and avoid the common pitfalls many executive coaches face in gathering feedback for leaders.

What Sets This Book Apart?

As mentioned in the preface, our literature review revealed no resource on executive coaching engagements that specifically detailed a framework of all the steps necessary for effectively conducting and leveraging stakeholder feedback interviews, while addressing both the trust needed and the management of emotional undercurrents.

The Feedback Framework

The Stakeholder Feedback Framework emerged from our experiences as a team, combined with what we found to be gaps in the literature. The framework is an easy to follow, step-by-step model of the main steps that are required to conduct an artful, actionable stakeholder feedback process. The Stakeholder Feedback Framework is based upon the following principles:

▶ Feedback is collected through interviews, not via quantitatively scored (often online) surveys.
▶ The coach and the leader co-create the questions about the leader with the goal of helping the leader develop.
▶ Stakeholder feedback is developmental in nature and is not intended to be used for evaluation.
▶ The goals the leader is working toward are focused on the leader being the best leader they can be and not solely on the organization's goals or performance competencies.

▶ Emotional safety is a critical part of how the coach collects feedback and how the coach and leader work together for the leader to make needed changes.

This book offers a detailed framework, tips, and best practices for coaches to collect, analyze, and deliver feedback as part of an executive leadership coaching engagement.

The Role of Emotions

Throughout the guidebook, we have inserted stories demonstrating the framework in action, to illustrate how the steps work and what role emotions might play. This book addresses the mindset and presence you need as a coach—how you "show up" for your clients—as you embark on designing and delivering stakeholder feedback in a coaching relationship.

As you read, keep in mind your favorite types of leaders as well as the most challenging situations you have encountered while coaching them. Start figuring out what role your emotions, self-awareness, ability to self-manage, and empathy have played in both your successes and challenges.

Breathing Life into It: The Framework Applied in a Typical Leadership Coaching Engagement

We mentioned at the beginning of this introduction that stakeholders are both signal interpreters and the living, breathing signals of change for a leader. We use recurring vignettes throughout the book of a fictional coach engaged to coach two fictional leaders, to show how each must negotiate emotions, self-awareness, the ability to self-manage, and empathy in their respective coaching engagements.

Introducing Executive Coach Greta and Leaders Sue and Richard

We introduce you to an external executive coach—"Greta"—who serves as our guide through the steps we teach for applying the Feedback Framework. Greta is a Master Coach who not only exhibits some best practices but also falls into some pitfalls where she misses a few elements of the framework. In the vignettes sprinkled throughout this guidebook, two different organizations have engaged Greta to coach two different leaders. As we narrate the scenarios, we will explore Greta's emotions as well as those of the leaders she is coaching and examine how she manages emotions throughout the feedback process. At critical points, we will give you some examples of both bad and good coaching (indicated by thumbs-up or thumbs-down icons).

Next, we introduce you to two leaders in very different industries, whom we call "Sue" and "Richard." Greta will illustrate each step of the Feedback Framework in her coaching of these two hypothetical leaders.

The following is a sneak preview of each leader.

One of the leaders Greta is coaching is Sue, a vice president of an international consulting firm. Sue has regularly been promoted throughout the years, yet has stayed at the same level for some time now. She has voluntarily approached her boss, Priya Das, to seek out coaching. Her overall objective is to grow in her leadership and demonstrate to her boss that she is ready for promotion to the next level. Sue has identified her own coaching goals to include (1) growing her leadership skills, (2) working more effectively with peers in a collaborative way, and (3) becoming more approachable to and supportive of her direct reports.

Another leader being coached is Richard, a neurosurgeon and, prior to a recent merger, the Chief Medical Officer of a large healthcare organization. The new CEO, Dr. Jin Lei, has just informed Richard that there have been several complaints about his directive, "abrasive" command-and-control leadership style. Richard has been told he must receive executive coaching. Richard's overall objective is to reclaim his position as Chief Medical Officer. The CEO's desired coaching goals for him? They are to (1) lead and communicate more effectively with other practice group heads and leaders, and (2) increase his emotional intelligence by expanding his awareness and management of his emotions and impact on others.

Both of these leaders have their respective challenges and pose different emotional scenarios for Greta to manage. You, our readers, in following the story of each leader, will discover how Greta applies the Feedback Framework to these two coaching situations while managing the emotional undercurrents throughout.

Chapter by Chapter: How Do You Use This Guidebook?

We recommend you read the entire book from cover to cover in sequence, as each step builds on the prior one. While the framework is sequential in nature, some steps may be more familiar to you than others, so you may want to take a deeper dive into those steps that present more of a challenge to you.

For example, if you are just starting to incorporate the use of stakeholder feedback in your coaching relationships, then you probably want to start with chapter 1, which covers the foundational elements of building a working alliance (between coach and leader) and coaching presence (through self-awareness and management of your own emotions). Or, if stakeholder interviews have already become part of your routine, yet you sometimes encounter surprising resistance to feedback (the giving and receiving of it), chapter 1 can help you with some of the nuances of the coach-leader working alliance and coaching presence.

If you sometimes face challenges in helping leaders discover their purpose in gathering feedback, and aligning it with the organization's goals, you will want to make sure to review chapters 2 and 3, which cover the bases of confidentiality, purpose, and the initial alignment meeting between coach, leader, and the leader's supervisor (when applicable to the coaching engagement).

If you get bogged down in scheduling and administrative details or want to find out how to structure the process so that it goes more smoothly, then go to chapters 4 and 6 on the administrative process and the writing of the report. We also include sample emails and templates in the appendixes.

If you face challenges in drawing out actionable feedback from stakeholders, then read chapter 5 on conducting the interview. An important part of this step is separating perception from fact. In this chapter, we share some sample questions for you to ask the stakeholders, as well as questions for you to ponder as a coach.

If you struggle with how to present difficult feedback in a debrief with the leader you are coaching, then read chapter 7. Our stories of two very different types of leaders, Sue and Richard, reveal that each leader comes with their own emotional reactions to feedback. We ask probing questions so you too can imagine what emotions might be lurking under the surface in these scenarios.

Perhaps you have a strong comfort level with conducting stakeholder feedback interviews, although you struggle with motivating the leaders you coach to create their own written action plans for incorporating the feedback. Chapter 8 offers tips and tools for action planning, supplemented by sample development plan templates in the appendixes.

At the end of each chapter is a Feedback Framework "Guidepost" containing some highlights about the step covered in the chapter. These lists will move you forward and help you synthesize what you have just learned.

Consider what you are most curious about with respect to this process, and let's begin our journey. As fellow coaches and leaders, we hope you enjoy reading this guidebook as much as we enjoyed creating it. We hope you benefit from it and develop your own unique style in applying the framework as you gather feedback for the leaders you coach.

CHAPTER ONE
Overview of the Stakeholder Feedback Framework

*"To become more effective and fulfilled at work, people need
a keen understanding of their impact on others and the
extent to which they're achieving their goals in their working
relationships. Direct feedback is the most efficient way for
them to gather this information and learn from it."*

—Ed Batista, "Building a Feedback-Rich Culture"

What kind of situation gives rise to the need for a stakeholder feedback process? It all begins with a leader's desire for professional growth. Recall the metaphor of a signal exchange for the feedback process, set forth in the introduction. Executive coaching provides a forum for a leader to become more aware of the signals they transmit and receive—an awareness that is critical to a leader's pursuit of their development goals. Yet if leaders and their coaches are not tuned in to multiple channels, they can miss valuable signals about how they are perceived by others. This lack of external input can result in a leader having blind spots so they do not notice when they get their wires crossed with others or unintentionally behave in ways that do not serve them well.

Take for example the leader who, wanting to be collaborative, asks others for opinions and then disregards that input in making decisions. The leader's behavior undercuts their own goal of collaborative leadership, as those involved become cynical about being meaningfully included. This is an example of a leader who would benefit from collecting insights from their stakeholders to help them understand how to better achieve their goals.

Executive coaches can help leaders embrace the stakeholder feedback process by igniting the leader's curiosity about how others see them. The coach can also facilitate the opening of the right kind of channels for signal reception and transmission through a co-created stakeholder feedback process. The leader would be an active participant in the discovery of these channels.

The stakeholder feedback process is only one part of the coaching engagement, and can occur at any opportune time, including at the beginning. When conducted early in the coaching engagement, the stakeholder feedback may signal the types of changes that form the foundation for the initial goals of the engagement. In cases where the feedback process is initiated midway through the coaching, the engagement goals will already be established and the stakeholder feedback will inform how the leader experiments with behavior change. The coach and the leader need to align on both the purpose of stakeholder feedback and how that feedback supports the broader coaching engagement goals.

When we thought about the steps that would be needed to communicate this process, we struggled with two things: (1) codifying the steps and their sequential order and (2) making sure the steps would allow for flexibility in how individual coaches used them. We thought about a process that would be easy to learn while also being adaptable. It came down to seven key steps for conducting the stakeholder feedback process (see figure 1)—each step is essential, and within each step there is room for individual coaches to assert their preferences, interpretations, and sense of self.

There are two foundational elements that surround the seven steps: the coach-leader working alliance and the coach's presence. Ensuring these two elements of working alliance and coaching presence are in place is the cornerstone to the effectiveness of every stakeholder feedback process.

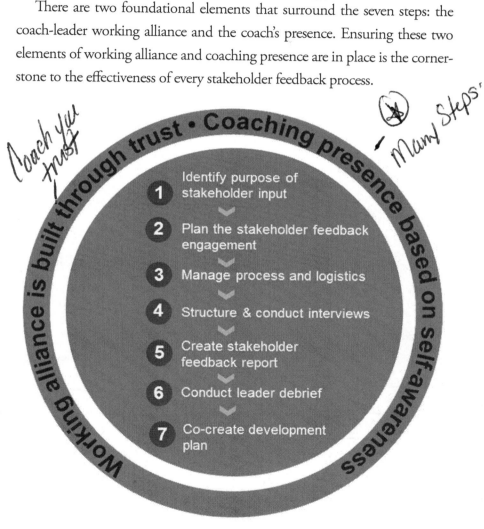

Visit www.fearlessfeedbackguide.com to download the full-color framework.

Figure 1[4]

---

4 See Appendix A, Stakeholder Feedback Framework with Substeps, for a more detailed version.

27

Two Foundational Elements Underlying All Steps

Two elements are foundational to all seven steps of the stakeholder feedback process: the working alliance and coaching presence. What we mean by coaching presence is the coach managing their own feelings, reactions, and thoughts through self-awareness. The non-judgmental collection, synthesis, and application of stakeholder feedback relies on constant attention to these two foundational elements.

First Foundational Element: Working Alliance Built Through Trust

Leaders often experience anxiety when embarking on the stakeholder feedback process with their coach. We are human, though maybe less willingly or openly so in the places where we work. Leaders experience even greater anxiety when the coach has been assigned, as happens in many leadership development programs. Whether the leader chooses or is assigned a coach, the coach must recognize that collecting feedback about the leader from their stakeholders creates vulnerability and triggers a number of emotions—including fear, defensiveness, or even outright anger. It is critical for the coach to establish a working alliance with the leader—one built on trust and an emotionally safe environment.

What do we mean by "working alliance"? We mean an unwritten mutual trust and acceptance that is entered into on faith (the coach and leader will be strangers to each other at first) and strengthened through the work of coaching. Without this working alliance, mutual learning is likely to be impeded. The leader must trust and believe the coach has their best interests, well-being, and success at heart. The leader must let go of their desire to manage their image and have everything under control and instead be willing to be a bit vulnerable.

In the preface, we mentioned our experience in the Master Coach Program and how that experience was, in part, one of vulnerability. What we learned about the working alliance was that it was critical to have a foundation of trust. Otherwise, it is too difficult for the leader to feel comfortable having the coach even reach out to the leader's stakeholders. A critical part of building that working alliance is ensuring that the coach and the leader understand the leader's purpose—both in pursuing coaching and in seeking out feedback in the first place. The following vignette is one example of how the coach and leader can get on the same wavelength.

Breathing Life into It: A Vignette for Building the Working Alliance

To illustrate the first foundational element of the working alliance, we turn now to Greta, an external executive coach who's been engaged by a large healthcare system that just went through a mega-merger. Greta's been retained to coach a number of leaders and healthcare providers in the system to navigate the transition. Richard is one of those leaders.

As mentioned in the introduction, Richard is a talented, brilliant, and hard-charging neurosurgeon who was also Chief Medical Officer at his medical institution prior to the merger. He leapfrogged over many colleagues more senior than he was to become promoted. He had his eyes set on becoming the next CEO before the merger happened. However, the very qualities that make Richard excel as a surgeon seem to be getting in the way of his effectiveness as a leader. He's driven, task-oriented, and decisive, projecting a commanding presence in surgery. After Richard became Chief Medical Officer, the former CEO received numerous complaints about Richard's directive leadership and communication style from other physicians and leaders. Complaints included "arrogant," "intimidating," "controlling," "dismissive," and "demeaning."

The new CEO of the merged organization (Dr. Jin Lei) has required that Richard receive executive coaching if he wants to be eligible for any type of leadership position (much less be considered for Chief Medical Officer). It is unclear how much Richard has been told about the complaints, other than that he needs to "change his leadership style."

In this moment, Greta and Richard are midway through their first coaching session, and she is just covering the role that stakeholder interviews will play in the coaching process. The italicized text (circled with dotted lines and thought bubbles) reflects the internal monologue of the character's emotions and thoughts. Recall from our introduction that the thumbs-down sign denotes an example of less than stellar coaching.

Greta: "I hear you saying that one of your key goals for coaching is to make the changes in your leadership style that are needed to position you as the Chief Medical Officer of the newly merged organization. Do I have that right?"

Richard: "Well-said. That's a good summary. So what's next?"

[**Richard's Hope:** *Perhaps this coaching won't be a waste of time if I get to hang on to the Chief Medical Officer position.*]

Greta: "One important tool to help a leader understand what needs to change is to get feedback from others about the leader's impact on them. So one of the next steps in the process is for me to conduct stakeholder interviews of your peers, direct reports, and supervisors to get feedback and insight about how you are perceived as a leader."

Richard: "What?!! Is that really necessary?!! And what do you mean by 'supervisors'?" (His face reddens, his tone becomes sharp, and his lips are thin.)

[**Richard's Anger:** *Whoa—who does she think she is, talking to others about me? Supervisors, ha! She's not even in the healthcare field—she can't possibly understand me or what my position is!*]

[**Richard's Fear:** *And what will she say in these "interviews"?!*]

Clearly, Greta needs to spend more time building a working alliance with Richard to earn his trust before going further. This will require a high level of self-awareness, compassion, and emotional intelligence on her part. She needs to notice the emotions driving his comments and leaking through his body language. Let's see how Greta reads Richard's body language (somatics) and reframes the stakeholder feedback process from his perspective.

Greta: "May we back up a moment? Before I explain what's involved in gathering feedback, I want to know more about your thoughts about this process. I notice just now a shift in your body, a sharpening of your tone, and a frown on your face. What are you thinking and feeling about this coaching, or about gathering stakeholder feedback specifically?"

Richard: "I'm really annoyed … and offended. After all I've done for this organization, I can't believe *I'm* being sent to coaching! I'm too busy for this! And as for feedback, my experience has been quite negative—usually it involves jealous, passive-aggressive colleagues who got passed over for promotion themselves, looking to dump on me behind my back."

*[**Richard's Anger:** Who do they think they are?!!]*

*[**Richard's Joy:** Whew, that felt good getting that off my chest.]*

Greta: "I understand—I hear annoyance and irritation. It seems unfair to you, and an imposition. What are your greatest hopes and fears about feedback?"

Richard: "Greatest fears are easy: I'm afraid of what others are going to think when they find out I've been sent to coaching. And I'm afraid of what you are going to say—no offense, but will you make things worse for me? As for hopes, I don't know; that I'll actually find out what I need to do to be the leader I need to be to become Chief Medical Officer again."

[**Richard's Anxiety:** *What if my enemies are out to get me, or the new CEO finds me deficient because of what he learns about me in these interviews?!*]

Greta: "Ahh ... three things I should have mentioned. First, your CEO has described this coaching as a positive investment in you as a high performer, not a remedial exercise. Second, the results of the stakeholder process will be confidential between you and me (no one else at the organization). Finally, you and I will tailor this feedback process to serve your goals and communicate the right message to your stakeholders. For example, we will co-create the feedback questions together and discuss the list of stakeholders. Would it be helpful if I explain the main steps in the process?"

Richard: "Yes, I'd like to understand more about how this works."

[**Richard's Relief:** *Perhaps she does get me after all...*]

Notice how Greta has mirrored back to Richard what she is observing, and how she has acknowledged his feelings to open up the conversation. If she had devoted more time at the outset to assuring Richard of the confidentiality of the process and building his trust by emphasizing how he would be involved throughout the process, the working alliance would have been stronger. And perhaps Richard's emotions would not have been so triggered in response to the mere suggestion of gathering feedback.

One thing to keep in mind is that the preceding example relies on Greta being present in person and noticing Richard's body language. We are not saying you must be present to read cues. If you coach virtually, you can look for signals in the form of tone, pauses, and perhaps asking the leader to describe body language. Whether in person or in virtual coaching, the coach can get help decoding these signals by asking leaders what they are thinking and feeling.

In sum, an effective working alliance between coach and leader must be in place *before* embarking on a stakeholder interview process and should be sustained *throughout* the coaching process. Remember, the leader owns any action that comes from the stakeholder feedback process and will be more motivated to embrace the process if they co-created it, which in turn means that they will continue to trust their coach throughout the process.

Second Foundational Element: Coaching Presence Based on Self-Awareness

In order to manage the stakeholder feedback process and conduct interviews in an artful manner, the coach must have coaching presence. Coaching presence has three essential facets: the coach's own self-awareness and management of their emotions, the coach's awareness and management of the leader's emotions, and the coach's creation of an environment of "emotional safety" that allows the leader to hear and take in the feedback being given. Above all, coaching presence requires a curious learner mindset: one that suspends judgment to pay attention to underlying emotions and listens for what is not being said. In order to cultivate this mindset, coaches must first be able to manage themselves through self-awareness.

A version of this self-awareness was coined by Dr. Pam McLean in *The Completely Revised Handbook of Coaching* as "self as coach" (2012). Here is an excerpt in which she defines this concept:

> [S]elf as coach: self-knowledge and the all-important use of self [are] the essential ingredient[s] without which effective coaching does not exist. Knowledge of self includes awareness and insight into our limits, assumptions, beliefs, biases, and blind spots that guide and restrain us in working with others, understanding others, empathizing with others, and more.

To manage the self, the coach must first be aware of their own mindset, biases, and feelings—both about feedback and about the specific leader they are coaching. Conducting stakeholder interviews, and delivering feedback, requires a myriad of "self as coach" skills from coaches, including, but not limited to:

- ▶ being present in the moment;
- ▶ being agile at handling the unexpected;
- ▶ maintaining a curious learner mindset, not a judgmental one;
- ▶ managing the emotions in their own tone and body language; and
- ▶ having the courage to challenge assumptions—their own and others.

The following questions are meant to help you build your "self as coach" skills or, if you already possess these skills, keep you mindful of the two foundational elements throughout each step.

Coach Questions for Self: Check Coaching Presence and Working Alliance

☑ Have I been present, listening with curiosity and suspending my judgment?

☑ Have I honored the leader's perspective? Have I met the leader where they are?

☑ What has triggered me? What work do I need to do to effectively manage myself in order to be fully present for the leader?

☑ Have I kept in mind where the leader is coming from, including "Are they new to receiving feedback?" "What context do they need?"

☑ Have I maintained an empathetic stance, remembering how I feel when I am the receiver of feedback or someone is interviewing my stakeholders?

☑ Have I been courageous and challenged the leader (and myself) about assumptions?

☑ Have I been aware of my own body language and that of the leader? If coaching virtually, have I been aware of the leader's tone and pauses, and asked about their body language when I want to draw their attention to somatics?

Coaching Presence Naturally Leads to Respect for Stakeholders

Coaching presence is critical to the way a coach transmits signals to and receives signals from stakeholders as well as leaders. When gathering feedback, the coach must be respectful of the stakeholders, yet mindful that feedback may say more about the person giving it than the leader, meaning that the coach must be aware that stakeholders each bring their own biases and motives to the interview. The coach needs to probe to get under these biases or motives, which is discussed further in later chapters. The coach must also be cognizant that their role is to seek, synthesize, and present objective data and insights, rather than provide their own subjective interpretation. To do this, the coach must be adept at noticing and managing their own biases and opinions (as well as those of the stakeholders) so they can be fully present to challenge and probe for facts and actionable behavior (rather than labels or judgments). We will say more about this in chapter 5, when we address the stakeholder interviews.

Breathing Life into It: A Vignette for Coaching Presence

To illustrate this second foundational element of coaching presence through self-awareness, let's turn again to Greta and Richard. During that first session after Richard's outburst of anger, Greta realized Richard reminds her of a former colleague with whom she had a number of conflicts in her prior career before becoming certified as an executive coach. First, let's take a look at the emotions and thoughts triggered in Greta.

> **Greta:** "One important tool to help a leader understand what needs to change is to get feedback from others about the leader's impact on them. So one of the next steps in the process is for me to conduct stakeholder interviews of your peers, direct reports, and supervisors to get feedback and insight about how you are perceived as a leader."

Richard: "What?!! Is that really necessary?!! And what do you mean by 'supervisors'?" (His face reddens, his tone becomes sharp, and his lips are thin.)

Greta: "It looks and sounds like you are angry! (Her face starts to flush and her volume rises.) What has been your experience with feedback?"

[Greta's Anger: Wow, does this bring back bad memories. I used to work with another guy just like Richard, and I feel angry and defensive.]

Next, let's look at how Greta exercises more coaching presence. She observes her rising anger and finds a way to manage her emotions:

[Greta's Shame: Stop, breathe. What did I do wrong to trigger such a tirade?!]

Richard: "I'm really annoyed ... and offended. After all I've done for this organization, I can't believe *I'm* being sent to coaching! I'm too busy for this! And as for feedback, my experience has been quite negative—usually it involves jealous, passive-aggressive colleagues who got passed over for promotion themselves, looking to dump on me behind my back."

Greta: "What was it about your prior experience with feedback from colleagues that made it so negative?"

[*Greta's Curiosity: I wonder about the motivation of his colleagues, and how that prior experience has affected Richard.*]

[*Greta's Compassion: Perhaps he's not just like my prior colleague. This must be frustrating for him.*]

What other emotions do you think might have been triggered in Greta? It's not easy to manage these emotions in the moment. Greta showed agility in dealing with the unexpected angry outburst. How could Greta have been even better prepared for, or even anticipated, Richard's reaction?

As Greta has shown us, coaches who have not developed the coaching presence and self-awareness essential to a "self as coach" mindset may have blind spots or even hidden biases. Such blind spots will likely interfere with their ability to read signals and gather actionable feedback, which could put the leader's learning experience at risk. It is essential that coaches develop a mindfulness practice of noticing and managing their own emotions so they can be better equipped to be in the moment with and empathetic toward the leaders they coach.

Working Alliance and Coaching Presence Can Catalyze Leader Self-Awareness

"Leadership searches give short shrift to 'self-awareness,' which should actually be a top criterion. Interestingly, a high self-awareness score was the strongest predictor of overall success" (Flaum, 2010, p. 5). This quote from a 2010 study of predictors of leadership success by Green Peak Partners and the Cornell School of Industrial and Labor Relations suggests that self-awareness is as critical for leaders as it is for coaches. However, unlike coaches, leaders may not be expected to exhibit, or even explore, self-awareness as a leadership skill. Stakeholder interviews provide critical feedback to the leader with the goal of raising the leader's self-awareness. While the coach cannot force the leader's self-awareness, by paying attention to these two foundational elements, (1) working alliance through trust and (2) coaching presence through self-awareness, the coach can model these elements for the leader. Depending on the leader's level of self-knowledge and blind spots they may have, examining self-awareness may be painful, threatening, or challenging. The coach must maintain an empathetic stance, create emotional safety, and proceed at a pace that meets the leader where they are.

Coach Questions for Leader: Build Leader's Self-Awareness

☑ How will we build our alliance to work effectively together? What do you (leader) need from me (coach)?

☑ How can we serve your needs by making careful choices about who I interview, what I ask in those interviews, and how the output of the interviews will look?

? How do we do this. Who actual coach?

- ☑ How are you feeling about coaching? About the stakeholder interview process?
- ☑ What are your concerns that would be helpful to discuss?
- ☑ What do you want to be sure we keep in mind as we co-create the stakeholder interview process and as you think about your broader coaching goal and your hopes for engaging with your stakeholders?

Pre-Step Discovery: Early Discussions About Past Feedback Experiences and Confidentiality

It is important for coaches to understand the leader's experience with feedback and establish the importance of confidentiality early on. Feedback and confidentiality are scary concepts for many leaders, and the leader's past experiences with feedback or their insecurities about confidentiality can color how they approach the stakeholder interview process.

Just as an individual's view of feedback impacts how they experience the stakeholder interview process, the norms around feedback at the leader's organization are important to take into account. Is direct feedback modeled at the organization? Is it possible the leader has never received well-delivered constructive feedback? Has the leader heard the same positive and constructive feedback that the coach hears from the leader's supervisor? Coaching is not a replacement for feedback from the leader's supervisor to the leader, and coaches need to be careful not to take on the role of delivering feedback that the leader has not heard previously. More about this topic in chapter 5, where we explore stakeholder interviews.

Confidentiality underlies all aspects of the coaching engagement and stakeholder feedback. The coach should discuss confidentiality with the leader and other parties involved at the outset of a coaching engagement. By establishing confidentiality, a coach sets the tone for all aspects of the coaching engagement. Confidentiality makes it possible to:

▶ clarify the coach's responsibilities to the leader, the leader's organization, and the stakeholders;

▶ achieve alignment among all parties involved; and

▶ manage the expectations of all parties involved.

As you read chapter 2, which addresses how the coach can involve the leader's **sponsoring** organization in setting the leader's goals and defining the purpose of stakeholder feedback, keep in mind that confidentiality makes those conversations between the coach and the leader's organization possible. Chapter 3 will go into more specific detail about how to address the confidentiality concerns that may be present for the coach, leader, organization, and stakeholders.

Coach Questions for Leader: Check Feedback Experience

☑ What is your experience with receiving feedback?

☑ Could you share an example of how feedback is typically given at your organization?

☑ Do you have any concerns about the confidentiality of what you have told me—for example, about your past experiences with feedback—up to this point?

☑ What are your greatest hopes and greatest fears about feedback?

It is important to:

▷ Recognize the essential role stakeholder feedback plays in discovering and addressing a leader's blind spots.

▷ Establish a trusting working alliance with the leader as a foundation for the stakeholder feedback process.

▷ Be mindful of your coaching presence throughout the stakeholder feedback process.

▷ Pay attention to your own attitudes and biases (as a coach) about the purpose of feedback.

▷ Explore the leader's prior experiences with feedback and the implications.

▷ Discuss expectations of confidentiality early on in the stakeholder feedback process.

CHAPTER TWO
Stakeholder Feedback Framework Step 1: Identify Purpose of Stakeholder Input

"Orient toward the client's purpose. Our knowledge of the client's purpose provides a foundation in the conversation. Orienting ourselves strongly to this makes us a powerful resource for the client."

—Doug Silsbee, *Presence-Based Coaching: Cultivating Self-Generative Leaders Through Mind, Body and Heart*[5]

W e mentioned in chapter 1 that stakeholder feedback can fulfill a variety of purposes. In this chapter, we will examine how a coach identifies the specific purpose of stakeholder feedback for each of the parties involved in a

---

5   Silsbee is the author of a trilogy of books related to the topic of presence. In addition to the book we quote from above, others in the trilogy include *The Mindful Coach: Seven Roles for Facilitating Leader Development*, and *Presence-Based Leadership: Complexity Practices for Clarity, Resilience, and Results That Matter*. Silsbee also was a valued guest faculty member of the Master Coach Program at the Hudson Institute in 2016, through which we authors achieved the Master Coach credential.

given coaching engagement. Coaches and leaders cannot become excellent signal interpreters without this critical first step. In the array of possible purposes, how does the coach help leaders and their sponsoring organizations define the purpose of feedback from their unique perspectives?

The first step in the Stakeholder Feedback Framework is to identify the purpose the feedback will serve for the leader. Three critical activities will help the coach and leader determine the purpose for collecting stakeholder feedback: (a) discern the leader's current state; (b) figure out what the leader hopes to learn from the feedback in service to his/her coaching goals; and, in situations where there is an organization sponsoring the coaching, (c) conduct a meeting with the coach, the leader, and a representative from the leader's sponsoring[6] organization (e.g., the leader's supervisor) to elicit the organization's viewpoint on the feedback purpose.

These are the three sequential substeps:

STEP ONE:

IDENTIFY PURPOSE OF STAKEHOLDER INPUT

A. Discern Leader's Current State
B. Align Purpose with Coaching Goals
C. Meet with Leader and Sponsoring Party

---

6 For simplicity, the term "sponsor" will sometimes be used in discussing the role of the sponsoring organization and the term "sponsoring party" will sometimes be used to refer to a representative of that organization (this may be a supervisor, HR rep, or another party).

A. Discern Leader's Current State

From the outset, it's critical to determine the leader's mindset and emotional state about feedback generally, and the role the stakeholder interviews will play specifically in the coaching process. Coaches must, in essence, dial in to the frequency of the leader being coached in order to understand their cues, signals, and gestures.

Feedback is scary for many and, as discussed in chapter 1, the leader's good or bad past experience with feedback can affect how they view the stakeholder interview process.

As leaders answer your questions about their perspective, you might find that they have had negative experiences with feedback in the past—instances in which their ability to transmit or receive was distorted or interrupted. In addition, leaders may be anxious about their coach talking to their stakeholders. Part of the working alliance and creating an emotionally safe environment is discerning the leader's current state and adjusting the stakeholder process to meet the leader where they are.

Coach Questions for Self: Discern the Leader's Current State

☑ What can you learn about the leader's current state by paying attention to their demeanor, tone, and body language?

☑ What assumptions about feedback are you as coach bringing from your own positive or negative experiences with feedback?

☑ How can you use the process of discerning the leader's mindset to strengthen your working alliance with the client?

As coach, we partner with the leader to create a lens through which they can effectively explore what they know, what they think they know, and what they don't know about how others perceive them. A further goal is to help the leader expand their capacity to hear, absorb, and apply feedback. Most importantly, the working alliance supports the leader to pay attention to and understand potential blind spots, as well as be receptive to acting on the feedback.

B. Align Purpose with Coaching Goals

An important first question to ask the leader is *What is your purpose in gathering feedback?* Sometimes it is to clarify goals or to raise self-awareness. Many times, the goal is to fill a feedback void—i.e., to gather more actionable feedback where the **leader's** organization has not provided any.

Coach Questions for Leader: Help Articulate Purpose

☑ What is your purpose in gathering feedback?

☑ What do you see as your leadership strengths, weaknesses, and areas to develop? How have these areas changed over time?

☑ What key challenges do you face and what feedback would be helpful in addressing these?

☑ How do you envision acting on the feedback you receive?

☑ What do you think your supervisor or sponsoring party would say they want you to accomplish with this feedback process?

Purpose and timing may intersect. For example, at the outset of a coaching engagement, stakeholder interviews can provide valuable data about the current state of the leader's leadership brand and the wider organization they are a part of; they serve as a source of input to the leader's development plan and coaching goals. Near the end of a coaching engagement, stakeholder interviews can provide insights on changes and progress the leader has made. In the context of an executive onboarding engagement, stakeholder interviews six to nine months after the start date can validate how well a leader is acclimating to a new organizational culture or flag potential issues.

These examples reinforce the signaling power of stakeholder interviews in the development of a leader. It is important to clarify the desired outcome with each leader and ensure alignment of feedback purpose with coaching engagement goals.

Let's imagine a leader who was told that to be promoted they need to improve their delegation skills and groom at least one team member to be their replacement. If this leader is unsure how to move forward with this objective, an aligned feedback purpose would be to learn about their delegation strengths and developmental areas as well as their ability to identify and develop future leaders. The timing would be early in the coaching process, which involves interviewing direct reports and others who have observed how the leader manages their team and workload. An example of a misaligned feedback purpose that leads to signal interference would be to have questions on topics that do not shed light on the two areas of focus, such as asking about their ability to influence upper management or their presentation capabilities.

In sum, stakeholder feedback will be most meaningful if the purpose is clear. The leader's coaching goals will help frame the right questions, the right roster of stakeholders, and the right timing.

Breathing Life into It:
A Vignette for Aligning Purpose with Coaching Goals

In these vignettes, our executive coach, Greta, is launching a stakeholder feedback process for another leader, Sue. As mentioned in the introduction, Sue is a VP at a large consulting firm who obtained approval from her boss, Executive VP Priya Das, to engage an executive coach to help her grow her leadership and demonstrate readiness for promotion. Sue and her coach, Greta, are about ten minutes into session three and are discussing Sue's coaching objective—to work more effectively with her peers and be more approachable and supportive of her direct reports.

In this "thumbs-down" first attempt, Greta obtains Sue's approval to complete the stakeholder process planning, but her "signal volume" is down—she is inattentive to the full framework and thus cannot hear Sue loud and clear.

> **Greta:** "Sue, in our last session we agreed to discuss how to best complete your stakeholder feedback process. When we discussed what you would like to learn from stakeholder feedback, you said, 'To ensure that the leadership priorities I am focused on are the most important ones at this point in time.' Should we start with completing the plans for your stakeholder feedback or would you suggest another starting point?"

> **Sue:** "Sure. Yeah. Let's get started on that."

[**Sue's Anxiety:** *Was it a good idea to request this coaching? What if something bad happens? What if I don't look good? Will this damage my reputation, my career?*]

Greta: "What do you envision doing with the output?"

Sue (frowning): "I will learn what others really think of me and can better show Priya my ability to work at the executive VP level."

[**Sue's Fear:** *What if there are too many criticisms and Priya loses confidence in my leadership?*]

Unfortunately, Greta cannot break through the static to accurately decipher Sue's emotions so she can tend to them and help Sue explore what they mean. There were missed clues, such as when Sue answered "Sure. Yeah. Let's get started on that" in a monotone voice, lacking full enthusiasm, or when Sue frowned when envisioning what to do with the stakeholder feedback.

In the following "thumbs-up" second attempt, the coach obtains Sue's approval to complete the stakeholder process planning and is more attentive to what Sue might be feeling and her sense of vulnerability in this process. Greta also helps Sue uncover her primary purpose for gathering the feedback.

Greta: "Sue, in our last session we agreed to discuss how to best complete your stakeholder feedback process. Because this process can make a leader feel quite vulnerable, even when it is in support of their career aspirations, I wanted to check in with you to see how you are feeling about all of this."

Sue: "Well, I feel somewhat confident that some of my strengths will be recognized and appreciated. I do wonder if I put myself at risk by asking folks to look at my weaknesses."

[Sue's Fear: What impact will this have on my reputation?]

Greta: "How is positive and developmental feedback typically shared and responded to here?"

Sue: "We do tend to be pretty open in processing our learning from each consulting engagement. We discuss what went well, how we helped our clients, what we learned, and what could have been done better. We do seem to expect that even good outcomes will have some rough edges and ways the work could have been approached better."

[Sue's Hope: I suppose that this might be true for my feedback.]

Greta: "Might there be any parallels between that process and your feedback process?"

Sue: "It's certainly possible that my stakeholders will not let the weaknesses take away from my good points just like when we do our engagement postmortem reviews."

[Sue's Optimism: There are some parallels here; perhaps this won't be as risky as I feared.]

Greta: "For you to have the most powerful learning from your stakeholder feedback process, how would you like it to unfold?"

Sue: "It would be great if I can confirm that I am working on the right things, both my goals and my leadership developmental focus. I am known for getting things done, and I want this to be true with my coaching. I also want to be open to blind spots that could impede my progress."

[Sue's Joy: It would be so helpful if I could get some actionable items.]

Greta: "Given what you've just said, what is your primary purpose then for having me gather this feedback from your stakeholders?"

Sue: "Learning my strengths and potential blind spots. I also would like to know what specific actions I need to take to accomplish my coaching and leadership goals."

*[**Sue's Hope:** Perhaps this feedback process can provide me the clarity I need to get promoted!]*

C. Meet with Leader and Sponsoring Party

For all internal coaches, and in many external coaching engagements, there is an organization sponsoring the coaching. The organization sends signals and also establishes the wavelength on which the leader is expected to communicate. In those instances, an important part of the equation is eliciting input from the organization on the issues they think are important for that leader's success. It is critical that the coach and leader communicate with representatives of the leader's sponsoring organization, such as the leader's supervisor and/or a contact in Human Resources, to reach mutual understanding regarding the leader's goals and the purpose of the feedback.

The rationale is twofold. First, in those instances where the leader's organization is paying for the coaching services (by hiring the external coach, or paying a salary to the internal coach), the organization may have strong expectations about what the leader's goals should be and what purpose the stakeholder interviews should serve. It's important for the coach and leader to understand and manage those expectations.

The coach and leader need to be sensitive to the fact that the sponsoring party will likely be evaluated on the effectiveness of the coaching investment. If the leader does not show change as expected by key stakeholders, the sponsoring party will have difficulty proving that coaching was a wise decision—and that will not reflect well on the leader or the coach. The sponsoring party needs to be sensitive to the fact that the leader may have aspirational goals that are somewhat different from what the overall organization and their supervisor request. It is important that the leader feels empowered and supported in their development efforts. Sometimes a leader will have a goal that is beyond what the organization has asked.

Second, it's often in the leader's best interest to make sure they are aligned with their supervisor and the organization on the coaching goals, the feedback process, and the definition of success. An important part of this equation is eliciting input on the issues the organization thinks are important for that leader's success. If the leader is not able to decipher the signals about what their supervisor or others desire, they could end up focusing on changes that are not considered priority items and do not create the traction desired. Take for example a leader that has been told to improve their executive presence. To the organization, this could mean speaking up more often in meetings with a stronger voice. If the coach and leader do not probe to understand the specifics, they could assume "executive presence" means that the leader needs to start wearing business suits and walking with confidence.

Equally important is clarifying with the sponsoring party the confidentiality of the discussions between coach and leader without the sponsor present. Although in many organizations it is expected that the leader share with their supervisor the overall objective and a very high-level status update of how coaching is proceeding, it is the leader's choice whether to share any detailed discussions or content from coaching sessions with their supervisor or HR; it should not be an expectation that the coach share this content. Without this agreement, it is difficult to establish the emotionally safe environment required for the success of the coaching relationship.

Of course, for some external coaches, particularly where the leader is paying for the coaching out of their own pocket, the organization's expectations may not be paramount, and the leader may not even want the organization to know they are getting coaching. In those instances, the leader may not want the coach to meet with their supervisor or HR (and, in some instances, the leader may want to forgo stakeholder interviews altogether).

This substep, which is only necessary if a leader's organization is sponsoring the coaching, is best accomplished with an alignment meeting with the leader, supervisor, and coach to discuss the purpose of the feedback. If an external coach is hired directly by the leader, this substep can be skipped.

Oftentimes, another alignment meeting as a check-in would occur midway through the coaching engagement, after the stakeholder interviews and some progress in the coaching has been made. It can be helpful to wrap up the coaching engagement with an alignment meeting to assess progress and establish a plan to continue the progress. Depending upon the organization and its structure, and how sophisticated their Human Resources function is, the meetings may be four-way meetings, with the HR representative, Chief Talent Officer, or the Leadership Coaching representative in addition to the leader's supervisor. In those circumstances, getting clarity about the role of HR/Talent/Coaching, and how they like to be kept informed, can better serve the engagement and ensure that it runs smoothly.

Breathing Life into It: A Vignette of Sharing the Rationale for Meeting Between Leader and Sponsoring Party

Let's return to coach Greta and leader Richard. He had no difficulty articulating his own purpose for the coaching: to find out what he needs to do to become Chief Medical Officer (again). However, he is balking at the idea of meeting with Greta and his boss, CEO Jin Lei, for an alignment meeting to discuss coaching goals and the stakeholder process.

In this moment, Greta is having a brief coaching call with Richard to discuss the rationale for the alignment meeting and to prepare for it.

> **Greta:** "As you know, our coaching engagement calls for an alignment meeting with you, me, and your boss, Jin Lei. Before we schedule that meeting, what concerns or questions do you have?"

> **Richard:** "I'm glad you asked. Remind me again why we are even meeting with Jin Lei? He's the one who decided I needed to have coaching, based on 'rumors' he'd heard about me that he had no personal knowledge of (and didn't even pass on to me)! Whatever he says is going to be tainted as he just has a bias against surgeons in leadership (since he's not even a surgeon himself)."

> *[**Richard's Anxiety:** What if Jin Lei biases my coach against me? What if his involvement just makes things worse for me, and he suggests stakeholders who have it in for me?]*

Greta: "Couple of things I should mention that might mitigate your concerns. First, I assure you the organization has not engaged me as your coach because you're standing on a banana peel! All their high-potential leaders are receiving coaching."

Richard (chuckles): "Well, that's good to know. What's the second thing?"

Greta: "Second, whenever an organization sponsors the coaching, I almost always talk to the boss, so we understand what the organization's definition of success is and get alignment on this process. I think it's best practice for coaches that we have that conversation with the three of us, so that you hear his views at the same time I do, and we have a shared understanding going forward."

Richard: "I guess that makes sense. I do hope he finally tells me what those rumors are that he heard. Maybe he will if you are in the room."

*[**Richard's Relief:** I think this coach is beginning to get me, and I feel like she has my back.]*

Greta: "So are we good to go on scheduling this meeting?"

Richard: "Sure."

As you can see, it's important for the coach to acknowledge the leader's underlying feelings about this meeting before it takes place. This conversation continues to build the working alliance and the trust between the two of them. Now let's see what happens when Richard's boss, Jin Lei, meets with the two of them. As you read along, see whether you can decode the underlying emotional cues each individual may be transmitting in this meeting.

Breathing Life into It: A Vignette to Illustrate Meeting Between Leader and Sponsoring Party to Align Goals

Greta: "Greetings, Jin Lei! I'm glad you could join us to discuss the goals for the coaching engagement and the gathering of the stakeholder feedback."

Jin Lei: "Certainly. I think this is an important part of the process, and appreciate you setting up this meeting."

Greta: "Having talked with both of you separately before, I think I have a pretty good understanding of what the goals of the coaching and the stakeholder feedback are. I'd still like to hear it in your own words to make sure we are all three aligned. From your perspective, Jin Lei, what do you see Richard does well that you'd like to continue to see him do?"

Jin Lei: "Richard's a very focused surgeon, and I can count on him to deliver excellent results for our patients."

Greta: "That's great. What would you like to see accomplished in the coaching?"

Jin Lei: "I'd like to see Richard improve upon his interpersonal communications and leadership skills."

Greta: "When you say 'improve on his interpersonal and leadership skills,' can you be more specific? What are some specific examples of behaviors?"

Richard: "Yes, I'd like to hear that too!"

*[**Richard's Anger:** It's about time he talks specifics! His passive-aggressive, indirect style drives me crazy!]*

Jin Lei (shifting away from Richard): "Greta, that would be one example right there. It is that sharp tone of voice and abrupt communication style that is off-putting. I understand many experience Richard as intimidating in his leadership style. That will have to change in order for his future success in the new organization. He needs to be much more collaborative."

Greta: "What are some specific examples that lead you to the opinions of 'intimidating' and not 'collaborative'"?

Jin Lei (continuing to look at Greta): "That's just it—I don't have specifics. Which is why these stakeholder feedback interviews will be so critically important."

Richard (blurting): "This is so frustrating! It's hard to make changes when no one tells me directly what they want changed. I am just a more direct person than most of my colleagues here in this region of the U.S. and, candidly, I am more direct than you, Jin Lei. I believe that directness is essential as a surgeon because it provides the clarity needed. That's a concern I have about this whole stakeholder interview process—if everyone insists on being indirect, I'm still not going to have clarity about what to change."

Greta: "I think you raise a valid point, Richard. If I may offer an observation, I have seen that the two of you do have very different styles in terms of directness. What I would focus on in the interviews is eliciting specific examples of when that directness is a strength of Richard and when it gets in the way. What do you both think of that approach?"

[Greta's Anxiety: I hope I haven't offended Jin Lei, but I do think that Richard makes a valid point—the advantage of directness is clarity, which we could use more of right now!]

Jin Lei (still looking at Greta): "I can see the validity of that approach."

Richard: "I do too. I'm curious about what examples there are of specific behavior people think I need to change as a leader to be more effective, especially as a Chief Medical Officer."

Greta: "So just to summarize, what I hear you both saying is that the goal of the coaching would be to make some changes to leadership and communication styles for more effectiveness; and the purpose of the stakeholder interviews would be to get specific examples of what those changes could be. Does that sound right?"

Jin Lei and Richard (in unison): "Yes!"

Greta: "And if Richard gets that type of specific feedback and could make some changes to be more effective, how could you as his boss help support his success?"

Jin Lei (looking at Richard for first time): "I would definitely support you, Richard. Believe me, I do see you as having potential, otherwise I wouldn't have recommended this coaching. I can't make any promises, but if you could become more collaborative, and find out what those around you need from you in that vein, you'd be a much more likely candidate for Chief Medical Officer."

*[**Richard's Excitement:** That's the first time he's looked at me directly since he got here. Perhaps this coaching is going to be a good thing after all.]*

What did you as the reader notice about the above exchange? How does the body language or potential cultural differences inform you of what emotions are lurking under the surface? Under what circumstances would you draw attention to that body language? Be mindful that part of this work is to strengthen the relationship between leader and supervisor as much as possible, as opposed to becoming the mediator in the middle.

Step 1 of the framework illustrates the interconnectedness of the goals of all those involved and the importance of continuity in looking at not only a leader's past experiences, present state, and future goals, but also those of the leader's organization. The context and alignment of purpose from this step will serve to channel now-visible cues into a plan for how the stakeholder feedback engagement will be conducted.

CHAPTER TWO
GUIDEPOST

It is important to:

1 ▷ Explore the leader's mindset and emotional state.

▷ Clarify the leader's goals regarding the purpose the feedback will serve related to the leader's professional development.

2 ▷ Clarify the organization's goals and feedback purpose (and have an alignment meeting if the organization sponsors the coaching).

3 ▷ Acknowledge the leader's vulnerability in having a coach talk with stakeholders.

CHAPTER THREE
Stakeholder Feedback Framework Step 2:
Plan the Stakeholder Feedback Engagement

*"Although we're generally drawn to like-minded people, it's
those who disagree with us—the ones who call us out, who
point out our weaknesses and flaws—who help us grow.
Those who challenge us truly make us better."*

—Justin Bariso, *EQ Applied:
The Real-World Guide to Emotional Intelligence*

As we can see from the vignettes of Greta coaching her clients Sue and
Richard, it is critical that, before planning the feedback engagement, the
coach build the working alliance, manage their own coaching presence, and
align on the overall purpose of the feedback. Now that these foundational elements are in place and the first step is completed, Greta can begin guiding Sue
and Richard through the planning of the stakeholder feedback engagement.

At this stage, the coach and leader must confront the challenges of figuring out what questions to ask in the stakeholder interviews, who to interview, and what will remain confidential. As the quotation above from Justin Bariso suggests, the most compelling insights about how a leader can improve often come from stakeholders who do not share the leader's perspective or who may be the leader's critics. As a result, designing the feedback process is not just a straightforward planning exercise; it's one which can raise strong emotional reactions. When leaders contemplate what areas of their behavior to investigate and what stakeholders might say, this can trigger strong feelings of vulnerability and anxiety.

A coach must be alert to signals of fear and related feelings from the leader in order to respond with empathy and to help the leader manage their emotions. The vignettes in this chapter will demonstrate how clues of the leader's emotional response may be visible in their facial expression, body language, or tone. However, sometimes the signals of emotional reactivity are less apparent and require the coach to probe deeper. One example is a situation where the leader delays identifying their stakeholders and uses excuses, such as saying they have forgotten or lack time. By exploring the leader's hopes and fears for the process and discovering what is getting in the way of identifying stakeholders, a coach may be able to surface a leader's uncomfortable feelings and help the leader cope with them.

By creating an atmosphere of safety, addressing concerns about confidentiality, and staying alert to signs of emotional reaction, a coach can use the stakeholder interview planning process as another rich learning opportunity for the leader.

This step has five sequential substeps:

STEP TWO:

PLAN THE STAKEHOLDER FEEDBACK ENGAGEMENT

A. Ensure Confidentiality
B. Agree on Timing
C. Co-design Questions
D. Identify Stakeholders
E. Understand Reporting Preferences

A. Ensure Confidentiality

To create a sense of safety for the leader and their stakeholders, the coach must clearly articulate at the outset how confidentiality will be handled within the stakeholder process, being mindful that the ethics rules of the International Coach Federation (ICF) set forth standards for confidentiality regarding communications about clients.[7] The ICF is the

---

7   The Confidentiality/Privacy Standards (numbers 24–27 of the ICF Code of Conduct) state, "As a coach, I...

leading global organization dedicated to advancing the coaching profession by setting high standards, providing independent certification, and building a worldwide network of trained coaching professionals.

The coach raises the topic of stakeholder confidentiality with the leader and shares the pros and cons of various ways of handling it. One way to encourage candor from stakeholders is by providing assurances that feedback will be blended together into a summary report in which the feedback is made anonymous and not attributed to any individual without their explicit permission. Alternatively, the coach and leader may decide that feedback will be attributed to the stakeholder who shared it, which may be an acceptable practice in a feedback-rich environment, and this has the advantage of allowing specific, descriptive examples to be shared without the need to conceal the source. Whatever form of confidentiality (or anonymity, if anonymity was agreed to as part of the earlier confidentiality conversation) is applied, it is a best practice for the coach and the leader to agree on how confidentiality will be handled with the stakeholders, and consistently convey to the stakeholders and any sponsoring organization what will or will not be shared. The leader should communicate how confidentiality will be handled in their initial request to their stakeholders to take part in the interview process.[8]

---

24) maintain the strictest levels of confidentiality with all client and sponsor information unless release is required by law.

25) have a clear agreement about how coaching information will be exchanged among coach, client, and sponsor.

26) have a clear agreement when acting as a coach, coach mentor, coaching supervisor or trainer, with both client and sponsor, student, mentee, or supervisee about the conditions under which confidentiality may not be maintained (e.g., illegal activity, pursuant to valid court order or subpoena, imminent or likely risk of danger to self and to others, etc.) and make sure both client and sponsor, student, mentee, or supervisee voluntarily and knowingly agree in writing to that limit of confidentiality.

27) require all those who work with me in support of my clients to adhere to the ICF Code of Ethics, Number 26, Section 4, Confidentiality and Privacy Standards, and any other section of the Code of Ethics that might be applicable."

The full Code of Ethics can be found at https://coachfederation.org/code-of-ethics.

8   See Appendix B: Template of Leader Email to Stakeholders Requesting Interview.

In addition, leader and coach must agree on who will see the compiled feedback report. Typically, only the leader sees the report and decides what parts of the feedback (if any) to share with others. For example, the leader may share themes with their supervisor or a trusted colleague who can support the leader as they make changes. In coaching engagements sponsored by the leader's organization, multiple people are involved (e.g., sponsor of the coaching, leader's supervisor, and/or Human Resources). All of these people need to align on who sees what before the feedback process begins. The coach should facilitate a discussion about what each person involved needs and how to meet those needs while preserving the confidentiality or anonymity promised to the stakeholders. For example, the leader's supervisor is responsible for delivering results to the organization, and the leader is a contributor to those results. Therefore, the sponsor and/or the person responsible for coaching must confirm the investment in coaching has an appropriate return. In these situations, the sponsoring organization may expect to see the whole report. The coach needs to ensure that all parties' expectations are shared and that the parties come to agreement on whether and how the feedback report is shared.

A third aspect of confidentiality is the coach's obligation to maintain confidences beyond the confines of the coaching engagement. The coach will hear many details about the leader, organization, and stakeholders, and must model confidentiality. The stakeholder feedback process and the coaching more broadly do not work if the coach fails to honor the agreed-upon confidentiality. This can be particularly challenging for the internal coach who may have ongoing interactions with the stakeholders. When the coach has other relationships with stakeholders, it is extremely important to clearly state the role of confidentiality in this process and reassure the leader that this is occurring.

Breathing Life into It: A Vignette for Ensuring Confidentiality

The following vignette demonstrates Greta planning the stakeholder feedback engagement with leader Sue. Sue is a high-potential leader who has the goal of developing stronger and more collaborative relationships with peers and more appreciative relationships with direct reports. Greta transmits and receives signals in a way that continues to build a trust-based working alliance with Sue and does so by ensuring confidentiality, agreeing on timing, co-designing the stakeholder feedback questions with her, and identifying stakeholders together.

Greta: "Sue, before we talk about the details of the stakeholder feedback process that we will be creating together, I think it is very important that we discuss confidentiality and agree on how to set this up to best serve you.

"There are two approaches to consider. One with strict confidentiality—comments are not attributed to stakeholders without their explicit permission, and it is worded to protect identities. This tends to ensure more candor from your stakeholders. Another approach is to report to you what is said in specific quotes or examples attributed to the stakeholder. This can provide you more specifics if you believe your stakeholders are willing to share in this way."

Sue: "I think the first approach is better. I want to be sure my stakeholders feel free to share whatever they have so I get the full feedback." (Sue frowns.)

*[**Sue's Anxiety:** I think I'm making the right choice here. But what if someone uses the confidentiality to take potshots at me that aren't true?]*

Greta: "Sue, that makes sense, thanks! I noticed your tone sounded uncertain. What's going on?"

Sue: "I just am a little worried about whether someone will take this chance to say negative things that I'll then have to report to my boss, Priya Das."

Greta: "Ah, I understand your anxiety. I assure you that your detailed feedback will be for your eyes only, and you will be in charge of whom you share details with and how. When I create your feedback report, I will take care to write it such that it does not reveal who said what unless I have their specific authorization to share a quote or example that would only come from that person. By keeping your stakeholders' comments anonymous, we ensure the greatest likelihood for complete honesty and transparency in the data that they share about their perceptions of you. You, in turn, have complete trust that the information is yours to use as you wish. It is your decision what information to share and with whom. This includes any summary reports or action plans we create. How does that sound?"

Sue: "I like that I will be in control of my destiny and can show that I am taking this process very seriously."

Notice how Greta clearly stated that the data gathered in the stakeholder feedback would remain confidential to Sue while also reinforcing the importance of keeping the conversations that she will have with each interviewee confidential. This anonymity is critical to ensuring that stakeholder interviewees present the most accurate and actionable data for the leader. Equally important, Greta also picked up on Sue's tone so she could discern any underlying anxiety Sue was experiencing about the process.

B. Agree on Timing

As mentioned above, the timing of gathering feedback from stakeholders is critical. The timing of the stakeholder feedback interviews should be examined from both a macro and a micro level. At a macro level, it is important to know if there is any noise or distraction in the organizational system or among any of the stakeholder interviewees. In the following vignette, Greta accurately reads Sue's emotional signals.

Breathing Life into It: A Vignette for Agreeing on Timing

> **Greta:** "Sue, the stakeholder feedback process can be a rich source of data for us as we explore perceptions of you from some of the most important people/relationships with whom you work. For this reason, the timing of gathering this data is critical. What, if anything, might be happening in the organization right now that could interfere with our ability to get the most objective and actionable data possible about your current performance?"

[Greta's Anxiety: I hope she understands the importance of this question and takes it seriously.]

Sue: "Our annual performance cycle starts November 1. So it would be best to get all the feedback in the next four or five weeks or else many of my stakeholders will be too busy."

Greta: "I feel that timeline is workable if you and I are able to design and set up the process in the next week, including identifying the stakeholders and you reaching out to request their help. What, if anything, might be happening in your key relationships right now that could interfere?"

Sue: "Well, last month I had a disagreement with my peer Anna. We formed a cross-functional team of people with representatives of my team and of hers to work on a project to streamline the bonus structure for employees. She acted annoyed with me that I was involved in the details, and I don't get it."

[Sue's Shame: I felt so judged by Anna that I totally shut down communication with her. It still hurts.]

[Sue's Fear: I am afraid to get her input when she is mad at me. This timing is bad.]

Greta: "That sounds like it was hard to hear. How did that resonate with you?"

[Sue's Indignance: You're darn right it was hard. I mean, who is she to judge me?!]

[Sue's Optimism: I like that Greta sensed that this is hard for me. She really seems to care about me.]

Sue: "Yes. I was only trying to make sure that the team got the deliverable right, and I did appreciate the work that they did. I felt pretty judged by her."

[Sue's Relief: It feels good to say that out loud and to have someone listen to me.]

Greta: "It sounds like there may be some unresolved tension between you and Anna. How important is it for you to have a strong working relationship with her?"

[Greta's Attention: I have a hunch that she wants to get this resolved and strengthen her relationship with Anna. I'm going to hold this loosely and see where Sue wants to take it.]

Sue: "Yes. There is. Our conversations have been stilted and uncomfortable ever since the day she shared her perceptions. Having a good working relationship is pretty important to the success of the team. Also, Priya really respects Anna's opinion. I'd like for her to think highly of me."

*[**Sue's Relief:** I feel relieved to say this out loud. I hope Anna and I can get to a better place in how we communicate and work together.]*

Greta: "On a scale of 1 to 10 (10 being high), how important is getting feedback from Anna as a stakeholder about your performance?"

Sue: "It's an eight."

Greta: "That sounds pretty important to you. Do you want to include her as a stakeholder?"

Sue: "Yes, I do."

*[**Sue's Fear:** I hope Anna doesn't talk about me to others in a negative way. And I hope this coach knows what she's doing.]*

Greta: "OK. Then we will include her as a stakeholder to interview. I'll be mindful of the tension that may come up, given the exchange that the two of you had last month. I'll invite her to be as objective as possible about the feedback she delivers and I'll consider that when I deliver the feedback to you in our review of the feedback report."

*[**Greta's Concern:** I'll need to be very conscientious about how I introduce this interview with Anna. I'll need to ensure I've created a safe and confidential environment for her to express herself. I'll also need to be mindful about appealing to her sense of objectivity and providing "data" that is actionable.]*

Sue: "Thanks, Greta. I appreciate that."

*[**Sue's Hope:** I'm really hoping she can get some good input from Anna. I trust Greta's instincts. She seems to have my best interests in mind.]*

Notice how Greta takes the time to ask if there is anything happening in the organization or among the stakeholders that could get in the way of obtaining the most accurate data possible. She follows her hunch that Sue wants to get her relationship with Anna back on track and invites her to quantify the importance of getting feedback from Anna by asking questions that require a response that is scaled (e.g., "How important is this to you on a scale of 1 to 10?"). Once she confirms how important it is to Sue to get feedback from Anna, she shares with Sue her understanding of the potential tension that could arise in her conversation with Anna and her intention to handle it with grace and objectivity. This level of transparency has the potential to further build trust in Greta's coaching relationship with Sue.

Exploring timing for the stakeholder interviews from a micro level includes a thorough discussion with the leader about what, if any, distractions could be happening in the work team (e.g., major projects, time demands) that could make potential participation in the feedback process burdensome to members of the team, the leader, or their supervisor. Finding an appropriate time for stakeholder feedback interviews gives the process the greatest opportunity for a successful outcome.

Coach Questions for Leader: Agree on Timing

☑ How long have you been in your leadership role?
If the role and/or the organization are new for the leader, more time may be needed before stakeholders can offer meaningful feedback.

☑ Where is the organization in their performance management cycle?
Stakeholder feedback is intended to be developmental, not evaluative. It can be confusing for stakeholders if these processes overlap, especially if the stakeholders the coach is interviewing are also the same people evaluating the leader's performance as part of the organization's performance evaluation process.

☑ What has recently happened in your relationships with stakeholders?
Be aware if feedback collection is occurring close to unresolved challenging episodes. For example, if the leader has recently needed to take an unpopular action in support of an organizational initiative, such as a downsizing of

the organization, it may affect the feedback process. On the other hand, it may be the perfect timing, so the leader can get insights into those relationships affected. It's important to explore these timing issues with the leader.

C. Co-design Questions

Once the purpose and timing of the stakeholder interview process are clear, relevant stakeholder inquiries often become apparent. Typically, the coach and leader will co-design the interview questions the coach will ask each of the stakeholders. Ideally, the coach will create a safe environment for each stakeholder to provide additional insight that the coach and the leader did not think of requesting.

Best practice is for the coach to share some generic questions with the leader as a starting point. The most powerful questions are often open-ended and evoke meaningful feedback related to the skills and learning edges of interest to the leader (see *Possible Stakeholder Question Areas* on page 79 for some examples).[9]

Questions about leadership competencies may fall into a few basic categories, such as:

▶ Leadership style/brand
▶ Creating direction/vision
▶ Managing others/managing up
▶ Executive presence
▶ Communicating effectively
▶ Inspiring trust

---

9   See Appendix C, Template of Sample Stakeholder Questions, for sample formatting of the stakeholder questions.

Possible Stakeholder Question Areas

Strengths:

▷ What are the leader's top three strengths? What do you personally most appreciate about the leader?

▷ Describe the leader's abilities: _____ [insert a list of specific behaviors on which the leader wants feedback]

▷ With respect to these abilities, give an example of when something was done well. Give an example of when it could have been done better.

Weaknesses/Opportunities:

▷ What gets in the way of the leader being most effective? What is the impact of that?

▷ Provide two or three suggestions that would make the leader an even better leader/partner. What could they start doing, stop doing, or continue to improve upon doing?

Future:

▷ Provide two or three suggested, specific steps the leader could take to be even more successful in the next twelve months.

In order to determine how many interview questions to include, the coach and leader should consider how much time is reasonable to request for stakeholder interviews and what portion of that can be dedicated to the questions, considering the need to reserve time for initial context setting and final comments. A typical stakeholder interview is generally

30–45 minutes in length, although some can run longer. Experience demonstrates that it's difficult to cover more than six question areas in a 30-minute interview, so the coach should plan accordingly.

In drafting questions, the coach and leader will typically want to elicit responses about both the leader's strengths and challenges. However, some coaches focus more on the positive, such as describing one or two moments when leaders were at their best. Another approach is to concentrate on questions that focus on desired future behavior and suggestions for how to improve, as opposed to dwelling on the past.

Breathing Life into It: A Vignette for Co-Designing Questions

In the following vignette, Greta works in partnership with leader Sue to design the questions that will be asked in each of the stakeholder interviews together. This "co-designing" is another means to ensure that Greta is continuing to build a strong working alliance with Sue and that she is keeping Sue in the driver's seat of her own development.

Greta: "We've talked about how important getting promoted is to you. You've shared that you believe that the opinions of others will make a difference in this decision. The most important people you work with are your stakeholders. We'll be identifying seven to ten people to participate in one-on-one interviews with me, and you and I will create the questions together. Before we identify those people, what topics would you like me to explore with these key stakeholders?"

Sue: "I'm interested in learning about how people see me. I'd like feedback that helps me get clear about what I need to do to get promoted. Also, I want to know that the leadership priorities I am focused on are the most important ones at this point in time for me. I want to get better at building strong and collaborative relationships with my peers, strong and appreciative relationships with my direct reports, and be in a position to be promoted to the next level of leadership."

Greta: "That's great, Sue. We can absolutely pursue those topics."

Sue: "Do you have any questions for my stakeholders that you can recommend?"

Greta: "Yes. I have some suggested questions to get us started. I typically start with two questions: 'What does Sue do particularly well?' and 'What could Sue do to be even more effective?' Then I move to specific questions that target your desired areas of inquiry and development. Earlier you said your development goal was to get better at building strong and collaborative relationships with your peers, strong and appreciative relationships with your direct reports, and be in a position to be promoted to the next level of leadership. What are some additional questions you might want me to ask?"

(Sue smiles, then immediately frowns.)

[Sue's Anxiety: Seriously, what are people going to say in response to these questions?]

Greta: "Sue, I notice your frown. Can you tell me what is going on with you?"

Sue: "Well, to be honest, I'm feeling a bit stressed about this process. I am nervous about the kind of feedback I am going to receive in response to questions on these topics. Getting promoted means a lot to me. I am scared that all this hard work may not pay off. I'm not sure I want to share anything with my boss until I find out what it is."

Greta: "I want to honor what you are saying right now. One of your strengths, Sue, is courage under fire. I wonder if there is a way to hold space for the scared and lean into the courage. How might the courage serve you?"

Sue: "I'm really good at leaning in to courage, and I think it serves me to focus on the positives. I have learned that I have a great deal of resilience, and when I let go of fear, I can lean in to new learning."

Greta: "That is really great, Sue! What wonderful self-awareness. Do you have more ideas about questions?"

Sue: "What about something like 'How would you describe Sue's willingness and ability to collaborate with peers?'"

Greta: "We can include that. We might also include something like 'What could Sue do as a leader to build even stronger relationships with her direct reports?' and as a follow-up, 'How might she effectively show her appreciation for her direct reports?' How do those resonate with you?"

Sue: "I like those."

Greta: "Great. Let's go with this list. Our next step is to have you share these with your leader, Priya Das, to get her feedback and support."

After having this coaching conversation with the leader about the topics the leader is most concerned about covering, the coach may then email a sample list of questions to the leader, which the leader will then edit and send back (see *Possible Stakeholder Question Areas* on page 79).

D. Identify Stakeholders

Based on the agreed purpose, coach and leader then explore the best people to answer the envisioned questions. It is important to collect feedback from the right stakeholders, as feedback is only as good as the source. In some cases, the stakeholders will represent a true 360-degree view around the leader (i.e., supervisors, peers, and direct reports). In other cases, it may not make sense to include all these perspectives and might be more important to include other points of view such as customers, suppliers, and/or board members. There is learning from those with whom the leader works well, as well as those with whom the relationships are more challenged.

Coach Questions for the Leader: Determine the Right Stakeholders

☑ Who has sufficient exposure and observations to answer the co-created questions?

☑ Who is necessary for you to be successful and for whom are you critical to their success?

☑ Who else needs to have input on the list of stakeholders (e.g., leader's supervisor/HR)?

☑ Are you including a range of stakeholder voices—including those you get along well with and those with whom you have challenges?

For many leaders, six to eight stakeholders will be sufficient to establish patterns. Others may identify ten or more stakeholders to be interviewed. The number is driven by the leader's preference, the culture of the organization, and the recommendation of the coach. The more participative the culture of the organization is, or the more complex the organization is, the more likely the leader is to request a larger number of stakeholders to be interviewed. Also, when there are known to be "camps" with disparate views of the leader, or when the leader believes different groups may have divergent perspectives, it may be appropriate to interview a larger number of stakeholders. Some coaches recommend at least ten stakeholder interviews for these reasons. Budget, however, may be a determining factor.

A smaller number of stakeholders can sometimes suffice for intact work teams, or a board of directors. It should be noted that smaller pools of stakeholders (less than four) can make confidentiality (or anonymity) more challenging, though not impossible. It requires great care from the coach to ensure no information is shared that could reveal the identity of the stakeholder participant.

Breathing Life into It: A Vignette for Identifying Stakeholders

Now Greta works with leader Sue to identify the people that she works with regularly who are in the best position to give her feedback about how her day-to-day performance is perceived. Together they identify the stakeholders who may have the most relevant knowledge to answer the envisioned questions.

Greta: "Now that we have agreement on the questions we will ask your stakeholders, it's time to identify which specific stakeholders you would like to be interviewed. Typically, stakeholders include your direct boss, selected peers, direct reports, and customers/key partners. It's good to include folks that you believe think well of your leadership and those that might find your approach more challenging. Would you like to discuss this here or reflect on the potential names and send them to me?"

Sue: "I'm comfortable identifying the names now." (Sigh)

*[**Sue's Fear:** If I include people that I don't get along with as well, will this slow down my potential promotion? What will my coach think of me?]*

*[**Sue's Anxiety:** Why would I want to take feedback from those people whose opinion I don't value or respect? They don't like me anyway.]*

*[**Sue's Fear:** What if there are too many criticisms and Priya loses confidence in my leadership?]*

*[**Sue's Optimism:** I'll have the opportunity to learn what others really think of me, and maybe then I can better show my ability to work at the executive VP level.]*

Greta: "OK. Before we get started, I noticed you take a deep breath. What are you experiencing right now?"

*[**Greta's Instinct:** I'm sensing some resistance here. And something seems to be going on with her emotionally. I'd like to get that out in the open.]*

Sue: "I have mixed feelings, as I've had some negative experiences with feedback before. There are some people whose opinion I strongly value, but others not as much. Also, I know Priya is really big on feedback, but I have seen her overreact before."

[Sue's Fear: This feedback process seems too risky, particularly with Priya and her inability to place the proper weight on big issues versus small ones.]

[Sue's Anxiety: Who are the right people to select? This feels important and unclear—what if I make the wrong decision?]

Greta: "I hear you. Choosing stakeholders can be a challenging process. I have had leaders worry that if they pick a few folks that are not their biggest fans, it will skew the result against them. I've also seen other leaders worry that if they only pick their fans, they won't learn anything. Usually, your critics bring up similar strengths and areas of improvement as the stakeholders who are more aligned with you. What concerns do you have about this portion of the process?"

Sue: "I want to get valid feedback that helps me get clear about what I need to do to get promoted. I admit I am worried that Priya will want to know more details than I will be comfortable with." (Pause)

*[**Sue's Fear:** How will Greta be able to manage Priya?]*

*[**Sue's Hope and Joy:** I can see where some of my bigger critics might really help me perceive my learning edges.]*

Greta: "What's your best thinking then about who would deliver valid feedback to help you get that clarity about what you need to do to get promoted?"

Sue: "Well, I definitely need to include my boss, Priya Das. I think we should also include some of my peers. In addition to Anna, let's include Dorothy and Steve. My direct reports should include Eva, Elaine, and Ricardo, and my customers/clients should include Rajeev, Michelle, and Bob."

Greta: "That sounds great, Sue. Are those the most important stakeholders to you?"

Sue: "Yes. Definitely."

Greta: "Then let's go with those. I'll send you a one-page summary of the questions we created and the individuals we identified as stakeholders. Please review that and let me know if you have any edits or changes. Once we have your agreement, I invite you to share the final summary with Priya Das for her input and agreement. Then we can start the process of scheduling interviews."

Notice how Greta keeps the focus on the people that Sue wants to include and on the goals Sue wants to accomplish. She also reinforces at the end the importance of getting input on both the interview questions and the list of stakeholders to interview from her boss, Priya Das. This is an important step in keeping the sponsor informed and in building trust and transparency about Sue's development between Sue and Priya.

E. Understand Reporting Preferences

There are many ways to present the feedback, and it is important to explore the leader's unique reporting preferences early in the feedback process. Is the leader a big picture, strategic person? Do they like details? Do they prefer a bullet-point summary? All these factors come into play when considering the design of the feedback report and how that affects the structuring of the stakeholder interviews. The important thing to remember is that the purpose of the feedback report is to raise the leader's awareness about the themes or areas of development that exist so that they may incorporate that information into the coaching, and in their development plan. The feedback report also identifies strengths that they can leverage to help them achieve their coaching and developmental goals.

Example of Reporting Preferences in Action

Let's take the case of a leader who is a financial services executive. Imagine this leader is responsible for a major transformational change initiative to redefine the physical plant of the company headquarters. The budget and scope of the work is in the hundreds of millions. The role is highly visible at the Senior Team and Board levels. He feels significant responsibility to deliver this work on time and on budget. He has questions about how he is performing as the leader of this critically important initiative.

His coach works with him to create and implement a stakeholder feedback process. Because transformative change will be most effective with leaders who model open, candid communication, he and his coach decide that it would be best if they do not promise confidentiality to the stakeholders. Before conducting the stakeholder interviews, the coach meets with the leader to ask if he has any preferences regarding how the report will be designed. The leader indicates that he would like an executive summary in the front of the document and then as many quotes as possible organized by question.

Given the leader's preferences, his coach needs to make certain to accurately record notes of quotes along with who said them, under each question, so that she is better able to design the report as requested.

Coach Questions for Leader: Discern Reporting Preferences

☑ What is your learning style (e.g., auditory or visual) and how do you ideally want to receive the feedback?

☑ How much detail would you like?

☑ How would you ideally prefer to see the feedback organized (i.e., by developmental goals, themes, or responses to each question)?

Coach Questions for Self: Check Empathetic Stance

☑ How is planning the stakeholder interviews impacting the leader? Have I noticed or inquired about the leader's feelings? Am I taking an empathetic stance?

☑ How has this planning process improved or compromised my working alliance with the leader? Have we created a true partnership in service of the leader's success?

☑ What am I experiencing? For example, am I emotionally triggered by my own experiences of planning for feedback or inserting my own biases?

CHAPTER THREE GUIDEPOST

To ensure confidentiality:

▷ Coach must address issues of confidentiality with the leader, the organization, and the stakeholders in order to manage the parties' expectations and comply with ethical standards.

▷ Coach, leader, and other parties need clarity on what information about the leader's feedback purpose and what aspects of stakeholder feedback will be shared and with whom.

▷ Coach and other parties must balance the leader's need for confidentiality and trust in the coaching relationship with the expectations of the leader's organization that they will have some input and oversight.

▷ Coach and other parties must design the process to balance the stakeholder's desire for confidentiality in order to be candid with the leader's need to get accurate feedback; this can be done by using general feedback themes and unattributed quotes.

(Continued from page 92)

In designing the process, the coach and leader need to:

▷ Select the appropriate timing for the stakeholder interview process considering the events in the organization and the leader's work.

▷ Collaborate to co-design meaningful questions given the leader's goals and areas of desired input.

▷ Select the stakeholders considering the need for a range of viewpoints and perspectives.

▷ Give ongoing attention to emotional safety for all participants in the stakeholder feedback process.

CHAPTER FOUR
Stakeholder Feedback Framework Step 3:
Manage Process and Logistics

*"Give me six hours to chop down a tree and I will spend
the first four sharpening the axe."*

—Abraham Lincoln

While at first glance this step may seem to be purely administrative, much more is at stake here than meets the eye. Along with Abraham Lincoln's great advice on the importance of preparation, we can add this popular adage oft attributed to Benjamin Franklin (another great leader devoted to change): "If you fail to plan, you are planning to fail." Which is to say, even in this step of the framework, signal disruption can still occur and planning is critical.

Start by answering the following questions: What's in it for the coach, the leader, and the stakeholders in managing this process well? Are there parts of the process where the transmission of what each party feels and thinks may be jeopardized?

For the coach, knowing that the logistics are in place and establishing the best interview mode to capture actionable, relevant feedback can make it easier to be fully present and self-aware in the interviews.

For the leader, a well-planned process can be empowering and can help build the working alliance with the coach (and stakeholders). This is particularly true if the leader invites the stakeholders to participate and makes sure they understand that their point of view is valued.

For stakeholders, it can help ease their potential anxiety about giving feedback. This is true as long as the purpose of the interview is made clear, the process goes smoothly, and the interview is scheduled in a way that is the least burdensome to the stakeholders' respective schedules.

This step has four substeps:

STEP THREE:

MANAGE PROCESS AND LOGISTICS

A. Establish Interview Mode
B. Set Up Note-taking Process
C. Initiate Stakeholder Contact
D. Schedule Interviews

A. Establish Interview Mode

The coach needs to determine in advance what interview mode will be used, as that will impact the process. Will the coach conduct interviews in person or via telephone or video? Conducting in-person interviews allows the coach to observe the stakeholders' behaviors, body language, and the organizational environment in which the leader operates, which is ideal. If the coach and the stakeholder are in different locations, this may not be realistic in terms of time and travel expense. Virtual interviews (including via phone or video) have the benefit of being easier to schedule and may make it easier for the coach to take notes. In addition to cost and time advantages, virtual interviews offer the possibility of using a headset and typing a more complete set of notes, whereas in-person interviews may limit notes to handwritten versions.

The unique circumstances of each engagement, as well as coach and leader preferences, will determine whether in-person or virtual (video or telephone) interviews are most appropriate.

B. Set Up the Note-taking Process

Consider how feedback will be collected—typed or handwritten—when deciding how best to capture the data gathered in the stakeholder interviews. Think ahead to how the data will be analyzed and reported to ensure sufficient detail is collected, keeping in mind the leader's reporting preferences. Above all, the coach should use a process which will enable an objective gathering of data, rather than the coach's paraphrasing, which might inject the coach's own subjectivity. Check the leader's preferences to make sure the process will work for them (keeping in mind that the leader's preferences should be considered as long as they do not interfere with confidentiality or practicality). For example, are quotes being captured in their entirety? How much detail does the leader want to see? Is the report going to be organized by themes or by the questions? How does this align with the confidentiality commitment?

Some coaches create a template for the note-taking in advance of commencing the interviews. This can take the form of a spreadsheet or a Word document with the questions already typed into it. Key factors influencing the selected method for recording the notes will include how the coach best listens while taking notes, their preferred way of consolidating and making sense of the interview notes later, and the leader's expectations about the level of detail they will be receiving in the written feedback report.

C. Initiate Stakeholder Contact

Ideally, it is the leader who initiates the stakeholder feedback process to gain stakeholder buy-in and set the tone for the feedback process. Typically, the leader will first ask each stakeholder if they will participate, informing them broadly of the purpose of gathering feedback. Then, the leader will send an introductory email to both the stakeholder and the coach,[10] who follows up to schedule interviews. The leader's openness to candid feedback and their desire to improve their leadership sets the stage for the coach to obtain clear and actionable feedback. This openness and desire to improve may also ease any concerns stakeholders could have about being forthcoming with the coach. Equally important,

---

10   See Appendix B: Template of Leader Email to Stakeholders Requesting Interview.

the leader's initiation of the process builds the working alliance with the coach and helps alleviate any potential anxiety the leader might feel about their lack of control over the process.

What happens if the leader is not involved in initiating the stakeholder contact? One downside is that the stakeholder may assume the leader is being coached involuntarily. They may be clueless about why they are meeting with the coach, and uncomfortable being candid with a coach they haven't met before. Another is that the coach may have to take valuable time in each interview explaining to the stakeholder what the purpose of the interview is and assuring them that the leader is part of the process.

D. Schedule Interviews

Once the leader introduces the stakeholders to the coach with an email, the coach begins the scheduling process. Some coaches schedule directly with stakeholders, others rely on assistants.

With scheduling, consider the cadence of the interviews. Will conducting all interviews in a narrow window of time make analyzing the data easier? If interviews will be conducted in person with several interviews in a row, allow time between to capture notes and insights. Gaps between each interview also ensure that subsequent stakeholders will not be kept waiting (and in waiting outside the door, overhear any of the previous interview). If this scheduling is not tended to with the convenience of the stakeholders in mind, it can negatively impact the relationship between the stakeholder and the leader and affect the integrity of the process.

It is good practice to send each stakeholder the questions at least a day in advance of the interview to allow for preparation. This helps stakeholders know what to expect and calm some of the fears they might have about giving feedback. Don't be surprised, however, if stakeholders have not prepared. Even when questions are sent in advance, stakeholders may not have had time to think about them.

Coach Questions for Self: Managing the Process

☑ Have I effectively organized meeting modes and locations so that they are optimal for my client and the stakeholders?

☑ Have I effectively communicated with stakeholders regarding this process and how their perspectives will be incorporated?

☑ Am I honoring the terms and spirit of my working alliance with the leader in my communications with the leader's stakeholders?

☑ Am I honoring the working alliance built with the leader as I prepare for the interviews?

CHAPTER FOUR
GUIDEPOST

It is important to:

▷ Consider the impact on the process when choosing the interview mode.

▷ Determine the best approach to capture information from the interviews.

▷ Ensure that the leader has messaging language to invite stakeholders into the process.

▷ Schedule interviews in a way that respects the interests of all parties.

CHAPTER FIVE
Stakeholder Feedback Framework Step 4: Structure and Conduct Interviews

"What we focus on becomes our reality."

—Sue Annis Hammond, *The Thin Book of Appreciative Inquiry*

F inally, the day has arrived to begin conducting stakeholder interviews. You have set up a note-taking approach in advance and you are ready to collect data on behalf of the leader. This may seem like a time for answers, but the Feedback Framework is first and foremost a process of exploration/deep inquiry. The quote that opens this chapter gives us our first critical question:

What will you focus on?

Let's be more specific (and in doing so, answer the question of focus). How will you ensure that the interviews are connected closely to the learning goals of the leader whom you coach? How will you obtain useful and actionable information?

A related and equally important question is: How will you make sure that the process of collecting data will be productive for everyone involved?

Before we begin breaking down this step, let's return to our definition of feedback from the introduction. We mentioned that feedback includes ***data*** (facts about the leader's behavior), ***emotions and impressions*** (feelings and assumptions on the part of the stakeholders), as well as the ***impact*** the leader has on others.

Although the interviews will collect emotions and impressions from stakeholders, your first check-in before beginning the work of the interviews should be with the emotions and impressions of the leader. You might ask the following questions to give the leader a chance to notice and name their own emotions and impressions:

▶ How are you feeling about the stakeholder interviews?
▶ Thinking back to our conversation about what you hope to gain from the stakeholder interview data, do you have any further thoughts before I begin the interviews?

Conducting successful stakeholder interviews requires three basic substeps:

STEP FOUR:

STRUCTURE AND CONDUCT INTERVIEWS

A. Create Interview Structure
B. Conduct Interview
C. Update Leader in the Interim

A. Create Interview Structure

Ensure you follow a similar structure for each interview by preparing an outline in advance. Here is a suggested outline for a stakeholder feedback interview:

► Open the interview, building trust and rapport.
  ▷ Thank them for their time.
  ▷ Explain the context of stakeholder feedback in the overall coaching.
  ▷ Ask about stakeholder's relationship with the leader: duration, frequency of contact, how and what they collaborate on.
  ▷ Discuss confidentiality.
  ▷ Confirm questions for the discussion.

► Ask questions to collect data, emotions and impressions, and impact.

▷ Use co-created questions specific to each stakeholder.

▷ Ask follow-up questions, asking for specific behavioral examples.

▷ Inquire if there is anything else to discuss.

▷ Determine if the stakeholder has any questions.

► Close the interview.

▷ Confirm with stakeholders that you have their approval to share examples.

▷ Thank the stakeholder. Assure them of the value of their time and input.

▷ Ask the stakeholder if they would be willing to be contacted if you have follow-up questions.

Once you have developed this outline, make sure to use it as a guide rather than rigidly adhering to it. One of the important aspects of gathering feedback from stakeholder interviews is to be adaptable in the moment. Let your outline guide you and be prepared to deviate from it if necessary so that you are capturing authentic, accurate, actionable feedback from the stakeholder being interviewed. Use your outline as a tool to get to that end; do not let it interfere with your listening or observing.

B. Conduct Interview

There are five key aspects of conducting a valuable interview:

1. Adopt an Active Listening Mindset

Throughout the interviews, active listening and observing are as essential as in any coaching session. These interviews should be approached with a coaching lens, so the coach can pick up cues as to what the stakeholder may be thinking and feeling. The mindset of active listening includes somatic observing of the body language, tone, and emotions of the stakeholder. The coach's goal should be to go beyond merely hearing the verbal content of the stakeholder's answers, to discerning the underlying meta-messages signifying meaning.

2. Establish Trust and Rapport

At the outset, establish an alliance with the stakeholder by creating transparency and trust. Start by thanking the stakeholder for making time for the interview and ensure the time still works for the stakeholder. Ask what context is helpful to the stakeholder about the role their feedback will have in coaching. Inquire about their experience providing feedback. As appropriate, explain the purpose for the conversation, referring to the email from the leader. The coach might ask, "What would it take for you to be comfortable being candid?" Set expectations regarding confidentiality/anonymity, providing clarity about attribution to specific stakeholders of any remarks, quotes, or examples. Invite the stakeholder's curiosity and questions; explore any fears or concerns they might have.

3. Ask Co-created Questions and Seek Examples

The majority of the stakeholder interview falls in this substep. First, discern the background of the stakeholder's relationship with the leader. The first question to ask the stakeholder is typically "How long have you known each other?" or "How often do you interact?" These are easy questions to answer, and they prime the stakeholder to become comfortable talking with the coach. In turn, learning this background helps the coach put the rest of the interview in perspective.

Ask the stakeholder questions co-created with the leader and seek concrete examples of the leader's behavior. Feel free to deviate from the questions, so long as you keep the interview focused on (a) the leader's purpose and (b) actionable behavior (as opposed to character-based assumptions). Often, stakeholders are unaccustomed to providing actionable, behavior-based feedback and instead characterize the leader based on their own biases (conscious or implicit). These biases may be based on perception rather than actionable behavior the leader can address.

This is an opportunity for you to coach the stakeholder during the interview. The first step is to notice any stakeholder comments that are based on assumptions, biases, or stereotypes about the leader's character and intentions. While discovering the stakeholder's perceptions is important, the coach will need to dig deeper to uncover the facts underlying those perceptions. Next, ask follow-up questions to elicit information from the stakeholder about behavior (as opposed to emotions and impact). Be prepared to ask curious questions about what led the stakeholder to make the judgments, assumptions, and conclusions.

These questions, and the stakeholder's answers, are an opportunity to recognize aloud what these statements really are (judgments). For example, if a comment like "she's intimidating" or "he's not a team player" is made, then probe further with follow-up questions such as:

► "When did you last observe behavior that led you to that conclusion?"
► "What did you see, hear, or notice about [leader]'s behavior?"
► "In the future, what would you prefer to see, hear, or notice that would be more effective?"

The benefits of using these techniques are that the coach is not only gathering actionable information about the leader's behavior, but also inviting the stakeholder to reexamine the basis of their perceptions and how they can perceive the leader's behavior differently in the future. The coach can also help the stakeholder understand how the leader's behavior impacts them by asking the stakeholder about their emotional state during the feedback process.

4. Take Accurate and Relevant Notes

Finally, it is critical to capture relevant, accurate notes during the interviews for creation of the feedback report. The better the interview notes capture what the stakeholder said (or revealed through tone and body language), the more objective and actionable the feedback report will be. At the same time, it is essential that the note-taking not interfere with the ability of the coach to actively listen and observe during the interviews, especially when body language or tone seems incongruent with the spoken words.

Regardless of which note-taking system the coach has selected in advance, it is important during the interview to maintain eye contact (when in person). Most coaches will schedule the interviews to reserve at least a few minutes after each one to capture nonverbal observations and insights. What was the overall tone and mood of the conversation? What nonverbal clues were observed? Were there any patterns? One approach that will help is to do most of the interviews within a few days to keep themes fresh in the coach's mind.

5. Provide Appropriate Closure

At the end of the interview, provide a sense of closure. The coach might check the accuracy of the leader's key strengths and growth opportunities which the stakeholder identified, using their words as much as possible. Ask if there is anything else the stakeholder wants to share or offer the leader. In wrapping up, double-check with the stakeholder to reconfirm their approval to share any specific examples and quotes with the leader (if that was the agreement at the outset). Ask permission to contact the stakeholder again if there is a follow-up question and invite the stakeholder to contact you if they think of something else to add. Finally, enlist the stakeholder's support in noticing and giving feedback directly to the leader as they observe changed behavior in the future. Thank the stakeholder and reinforce the value of their contributions. Finally, reassure them of the agreed-upon confidentiality.

Coach Questions for Self: Throughout the Interview

☑ Am I bringing a curious mindset and listening for hidden messages, noticing body language, and cues for emotions being felt or thoughts not being expressed?

☑ Am I open-minded and have I set aside any judgments about individual stakeholders or the organization overall?

☑ Have I respectfully probed to get below the surface to understand what is experienced by this stakeholder in relation to the leader?

☑ Have I focused on harvesting this stakeholder's perspective about the relationship and challenged them to see if there might be other perspectives?

Breathing Life into It: A Series of Vignettes for Conducting Interviews

In this series of vignettes, coach Greta is busy structuring and conducting multiple stakeholder interviews in the service of leaders Sue and Richard.

First, we will look in on her interactions with Eva, one of Sue's direct reports. In take one, Greta comes rushing into her interview with Eva immediately after coaching another leader due to a tight schedule. Greta is concerned that she should not have agreed to the other appointment prior to meeting with Eva. She is entering the interview without having fully prepared for either the content of the discussion or for grounding herself so that she has the coaching presence to conduct the kind of conversation with Eva that will build trust.

Greta: "Eva, thanks for meeting with me regarding stakeholder input for your VP, Sue. Sue is hoping for a promotion and wants to count on her direct reports to provide feedback that is helpful. Let's get started."

Eva: "That would be awesome."

*[**Eva's Fear:** Last time I gave stakeholder feedback, it seemed that my colleague knew what I had said and it made it very awkward to work together for months. And if Sue doesn't get this promotion, will she blame me?]*

[Eva's Anxiety: What does helpful feedback even mean? What if I'm not helpful?]

Greta: "All right, Eva. Let's start with what Sue does well."

Eva: "Sue is smart, she is able to get the hard things done, she is not afraid to speak her mind, she is well known throughout the company, and she is strategic. Oh, and did I mention she is smart?"

[Eva's Anxiety: I hope that is what Sue expects to hear.]

Greta: "What could Sue do to be more effective as a leader?"

Eva: "Gee, I'm not really sure. I mean, she is a great leader. I can't really think of anything."

[Eva's Fear: I am not going to mention Sue's temper. If she finds out I said it, I don't want her temper directed at me.]

Greta: "I am sure you can think of something. For Sue to improve, it would be helpful if you can mention one area for improvement. Sue said she really wants to be a stronger leader."

Eva (tentatively): "Well, people have said that she sometimes doesn't listen, but I haven't really had that problem with her."

[Eva's Fear: I wish she would stop pressing me. I'm afraid I'll blurt out something I shouldn't.]

Greta: "Is there anything else you think it would be important for me to know as her coach?"

Eva: "No, I think we covered it."

[Eva's Fear: Did I escape unharmed? Will Sue know what I said?]

In this alternative meeting with Eva, Greta has allowed for preparation time prior to the interview. She pulls out her Stakeholder Feedback Framework to remind herself of the foundational elements for the process and the key steps in conducting the interviews. She is grounded and feels ready to get to know Eva and learn from Eva's experience working for Sue.

Greta: "Eva, thanks for meeting with me regarding stakeholder input for your VP, Sue. I understand it can be tricky to provide feedback to your direct leader. I want to assure you this process is designed to use best practices, including keeping the comments made by each individual anonymous. I will not tell Sue any specific remarks from you unless I get your permission to quote you. The report will address the broad themes and needs to be written to protect your anonymity. Do you have any questions or concerns before we begin?"

Eva: "No, I've read the questions you sent out in advance and I'm ready to start."

[Eva's Fear: *Last time I gave feedback the person somehow knew, and boy, did I pay for that. I'm not letting that happen again.*]

[Eva's Joy: *It would be great if Sue could get feedback that will make her a better boss, though.*]

Greta (obvious display of active listening): "What does Sue do particularly well?" (Greta will take notes, be engaged, and continue active listening.)

Eva: "Sue is smart, she is able to get the hard things done, she is not afraid to speak her mind, she is well known throughout the company, and she is strategic."

*[**Eva's Fear:** I don't get to see Sue in some situations, so I hope this feedback is on target.]*

*[**Eva's Joy:** Sue does have some good traits.]*

Greta (chuckling): "Well, you went above and beyond with that answer!! Thank you! Let's move to the flip side. What might Sue do to be a more effective leader?"

Eva: "Sometimes she seems to get more upset than the circumstances warrant."

*[**Eva's Anxiety:** Should I have said that? Will Greta realize this means temper?]*

*[**Eva's Hope:** I sure hope this coach doesn't just hear this from me, as I have heard others mention Sue's temper many times before.]*

Greta: "Could you help me understand what 'getting more upset than circumstances warrant' looks like by describing a recent example where this occurred?"

Eva (tentatively): "Well, we were in a team meeting and I reported that a key project was running behind schedule. Before I had the chance to discuss what was being done to get it back on track, Sue interrupted and said that this project was critically important and she can't believe I let it slip like that. I wanted to shrink into my chair. I was unable to share more important information because she derailed the meeting."

*[**Eva's Fear:** Boy, did that upset me.]*

*[**Eva's Joy:** It does feel good to get that off my chest.]*

Greta: "I notice your tone grew louder at the end there. What did you notice about Sue's tone and body language in that meeting?"

Eva: "She got louder than I did just now, and was frowning at me."

Greta: "Hmm, what happened next?"

Eva: "Sue moved on to another agenda item, and I sent her an email after the meeting to assure her that I felt confident the project would finish on time with the corrective actions I was taking. I never heard anything back. Can you believe that? I feel she owes me an apology for calling me out in front of my peers like that and for yelling at me."

*[**Eva's Joy**: I sure hope Sue can learn to manage her quick fuse better.]*

Greta: "Thank you for providing this specific example that creates such clarity around this area of potential growth for Sue. When I create the stakeholder report, I will ensure that it is included in a way that is not attributable to you."

Coach Questions for Self: Conducting the Interviews

☑ Am I prepared for each interview, yet ready to flex if the situation requires that?

☑ Am I fully present and curious?

☑ Am I aware and respectful of the work culture or system in which the stakeholder operates?

☑ Am I noticing the stakeholder's tone and body language to look for cues about the impact the leader is having?

Next, we will look in on Greta's interactions with Anna, one of Sue's peers. In one possible scenario, Greta shows up to meet with Anna feeling very present and ready to connect and learn. Unfortunately, Anna shows up late and says she is leaving town for business travel for the next four weeks. Anna needs to get this interview done with a hard stop in 15 minutes. This throws Greta off from the very beginning, and she is unable to either collect data or read any of the emotional signals Anna is sending out.

Greta: "Anna, I will do my best to get through this interview in 15 minutes. Sue mentioned that getting along with her peers is important to her and that it could help her achieve her goals. I promise that anything you say will be anonymous and only be used in the category of peer feedback so Sue will not know who said what. Do you have any questions or concerns before we get started?"

Anna: "No, I understand what this is all about."

*[**Anna's Anger:** Here we go again. Everything is all about Sue and Sue reaching her goals. I am so sick of hearing about what Sue wants. Sure, she wants to support others, as long as they play to her agenda.]*

Greta: "What does Sue do particularly well?"

Anna: "Sue is focused on her goals and what she wants to accomplish. She knows a lot about the business, as she has been here for so many years. Sue interfaces with executive management very well."

*[**Anna's Anger:** If Sue had her way, the Executive VPs would believe that nothing good ever happens around here without her magic touch. Makes me sick.]*

Greta: "What would you recommend that Sue do differently to be a more effective leader?"

Anna: "She could acknowledge others more."

*[**Anna's Anger:** Like that is going to happen. First, she would need to put her ego aside to see that others exist and that the last three project successes were actually completed in spite of her parachuting in to "save the day."]*

Greta: "What is an example of something you wish Sue would have acknowledged?"

Anna: "That's easy. Last month when we streamlined the bonus structure for our employees, she could have made it clear to the Executive VPs who made these changes possible."

*[**Anna's Anger:** I still don't know how the two people from my team pulled this off in the midst of Sue's interference. She is a total micromanaging meddler.]*

Coach Questions for Self: Getting Past Signal Disruptions

- ☑ What is within my control? If a stakeholder is late or has more limited time than expected, does it make sense to reschedule?
- ☑ If I think I need more time with a stakeholder, have I asked them for their agreement that I can follow up with them later by phone before we end the interview?

In this second example of Greta interviewing Sue's peer, Anna, Greta again shows up feeling very present, ready to connect and learn. And this time Anna shows up on time, ready for the conversation. Greta is happy that she is able to conduct the interview much more in accordance with the Stakeholder Feedback Framework.

Greta: "Thanks for taking the time to meet with me regarding stakeholder input for Sue. Sue mentioned that getting along with her peers is important to her not only for her goals but also to better support others and their goals. We really want to understand your point of view regarding what is working well and what could be better, including how Sue might support you. I promise anything you say will be anonymous and she will not know who said what. Do you have any questions or concerns before we get started?"

Anna: "No, I understand what this is all about."

[*Anna's Anger: Yeah, right. Sure, she wants to support others, as long as they play to her agenda.*]

[*Anna's Hope: Come on, Anna, this could be your only opportunity to make things better. Don't give up all hope.*]

Greta: "When you say that you see what this is all about, what potential outcome would you like?"

Anna: "If our relationship was better, I can see a positive impact for my team and for me. I doubt that is possible."

[Anna's Anger: Don't get your hopes up; you have been burned by Sue many times before.]

[Anna's Joy: It is nice to hear Greta say that I could benefit from this process in some way.]

Greta: "What causes you to doubt that is possible?"

Anna: "It is hard for me to imagine Sue leading in a way that is supportive of me and my team's goals."

[Anna's Anger: Sue's goals take all the air out of a room. Does she even see my goals?]

[Anna's Joy: If she knew that collaborating would help her, then maybe this is an opening for some change that is helpful to me and others.]

Greta: "I can understand that doubt. Your input is so critical to this process, and Sue really wanted you on her interview list. I wonder if you are still willing to offer your best feedback to her and share what Sue does particularly well."

Anna: "Sure. Sue is focused on her goals and what she wants to accomplish. She knows a lot about the business, as she has been here for so many years. Sue interfaces with executive management very well."

[**Anna's Joy:** *If Sue could bring even half the positive energy to others that she brings to executive management, things could be so much better.*]

Greta: "What one thing might Sue do to be more effective as a leader?"

Anna: "She could interact with others like she does with executive management."

[**Anna's Joy:** *I hope this coach reads between the lines and gets what I mean.*]

Greta: "I hear you saying that Sue does a good job of interacting with executive management. What does she do particularly well with executive management that could be leveraged in her relationship with others?"

Anna: "She treats them with great respect, she listens, and she honors their contributions."

[Anna's Anger: She is a total suck-up.]

Greta: "And how about an example where Sue did not treat others like she treats executive management?"

Anna: "Last month when we streamlined the bonus structure for our employees, she could have asked the folks doing the work if they needed anything and then backed off. We did staff this critical project with our high-performing people. Then she could have thanked the team members and told the Executive VPs who made these changes possible."

[Anna's Joy: If she could use her executive management influence for the good of the whole organization instead of just her piece, we could all accomplish greater things and enjoy this place more.]

Greta: "I sense that there may be more you want to share. Is there something else?"

Anna: "I hate to get my hopes up too far with Sue. She has behaved this way for a long time. It seems to be rewarded around here too. Will she really change? I mean . . . why would she?"

[**Anna's Joy**: Is it really possible this coaching engagement is a sign that the status quo is not what Sue really wants?]

Greta: "It can be hard for any leader to change when the organization is used to that leader behaving in a certain way. Having a support system can make a big difference. I wonder how you might be able to help her."

Anna: "If she asked for my help, I would be willing to try as long as she listens."

[**Anna's Joy**: Maybe, just maybe, things can get better!]

Breathing Life into It: More Vignettes for Conducting Interviews

Next, Greta interviews two of Richard's stakeholders, nurse Nancy and fellow surgeon Daniel. Learning from her experience with Sue's stakeholders, Greta has set aside enough time to center herself and review the Stakeholder Feedback Framework so she is ready to be fully present to connect with each stakeholder. This first vignette covers an excerpt of Greta's interviews of Nancy, who is a loyal member of Richard's surgical team.

Greta: "Nancy, thanks for taking time to meet with me to provide feedback on Richard. Before we begin, I wanted to put your mind at ease that everything you and the other stakeholders share with me will be confidential in that your responses will be anonymous; I will not be telling Richard any specific remarks attributed to you unless I get your permission to quote you. It will also be confidential in that the only person who will receive the broad themes of the feedback will be Richard, and it will be written to protect the anonymity of all stakeholders. Do you have any questions or concerns?"

Nancy: "No. Let's get going."

*[**Nancy's Eagerness/Joy:** I sure hope I can help Richard become Chief Medical Officer again! Wonder what he wants me to say?]*

Greta: "First, Nancy, can you give me a little context or background on how long and frequently you and Richard have worked together?"

Nancy: "I've been a part of Richard's core surgical team for the past thirty years, throughout both our respective careers. So I work with him on a daily basis ... I'm a big fan!"

*[**Nancy's Pride:** No one knows Richard better than me!]*

Greta: "Wow, that's a long time! What do you most appreciate about working with Richard? In other words, what are his top three strengths?"

*[**Greta's Skepticism:** Wonder if this stakeholder can be objective? I have to manage my skepticism here.]*

Nancy: "Where do I begin?! He's direct and clear in his communications to us as his team, so we always know where we stand and what we are to do, which is critical in surgery. Second, I am proud to be a part of his team, as he's the most talented, brilliant surgeon in the field! Finally, he's got our back—he always supports us as a team and makes sure we have the resources (and pay) we need and deserve."

*[**Nancy's Love/Admiration:** He really IS the best!]*

Greta: "I can see why you are such a fan! I hear (1) direct, clear communicator; (2) talented, bright surgeon; and (3) loyal, supportive supervisor/leader. Are those your top three?"

Nancy: "Yes, I think that sums it up nicely!"

[Nancy's Relief: Well, that wasn't so hard. Hope we're done!]

Greta: "Thanks. On the flip side, what is one thing Richard might do to be even more effective as a leader?"

Nancy: "Nothing I can think of—he's terrific!" (smiles, then frowns)

*[Nancy's Irritation: I'm really annoyed ... and offended. After all Richard's done for this organization, I can't believe **he's** being sent to coaching! **He** doesn't need to change anything. They should have that jerk Daniel in coaching!]*

Greta: "I noticed you frowned just there. What were you thinking just then?"

Nancy: "I just don't understand why Richard's in coaching and others aren't. He's so much easier to work with than some of the other surgeons—like that Daniel. So I don't want to say anything that would put Richard in a negative light, or give Daniel an advantage..."

[Nancy's Fear: Oops! Shouldn't have said that! What if that gets back to Daniel and he retaliates?!]

[Nancy's Optimism: On the other hand, I hope giving this coach some perspective will help her be less accepting about what Daniel's likely to say.]

Greta: "First, I just wanted to put you at ease, that all the leaders are getting coaching after this merger, so this is a positive investment in all leaders, including Richard. I assure you, no one else will be receiving a summary of this stakeholder feedback from me except Richard. So in that light, can you think of anything he could start doing, stop doing, or continue doing to be even more effective in the future?"

Nancy: "Well… he could stop interrupting Constance in meetings."

Greta: "Can you give me a specific example of that behavior and its impact?"

Nancy: "Sure. Constance is the chair of oncology. At our meetings, when she does speak, she seems to go on and on, so Richard often interrupts her. And I think when he does, she feels intimidated and then clams up. Frankly, I think she needs a backbone, as *I* don't think Richard's intimidating, But I do think it makes him look bad."

[Nancy's Anxiety: Ooooh… I feel queasy about this. What if this hurts Richard's chances of becoming Chief Medical Officer again? Will he blame me if he finds out I said that?]

What other emotions do you think might have been triggered in Greta as she was interviewing the ever-loyal nurse Nancy? What other questions could Greta have asked to gain more specific examples of areas of improvement for Richard as a leader?

We turn next to Greta's interview of Richard's stakeholder and fellow surgeon, Daniel. All Greta knows is that Richard was very reluctant to have Daniel be listed as a stakeholder, and only did so after the insistence of his boss, Jin Lei. What Greta is unaware of is that Daniel, who is more senior than Richard, is disgruntled and bitter about being passed over for the role of Chief Medical Officer initially and would like to see Richard fail. Greta is finding it difficult to translate the signs of what might be underlying Daniel's emotions and his comments.

> **Greta:** "Daniel, thanks for taking time out of your busy surgical schedule to meet with me to provide feedback on your colleague, Richard. Before we begin, I wanted to put your mind at ease that everything you and the other stakeholders share with me will be anonymous, in the sense that I will not be telling Richard any specific remarks attributed to you unless I get your permission to quote you. It will also be confidential, in that ..."

> **Daniel (interrupting, face red):** "I don't care about any of that. Whatever I tell you, I'd tell to Richard's face. Let's just get on with the questions you sent me, as I have more important things to be doing right now..."

[Daniel's Anger/Impatience: Richard is such an arrogant piece of work. I resent that I have to waste my time helping him by talking to this coach.]

Greta: "Very well. First, can you give me a little context or background on how long and frequently you and Richard have worked together?"

Daniel: "I've been at this organization several years longer than Richard, and in fact taught him everything he knows. While I no longer see him in surgery, I see him plenty in the department chairs' meetings, which he led as Chief Medical Officer up until the merger was completed."

[Daniel's Disgust: For the life of me, I still can't believe he was promoted to Chief Medical Officer!]

Greta: "Sounds like you have experienced him as a leader in several contexts. What do you most appreciate about working with Richard? In other words, what are his top three strengths?"

[Greta's Irritation: Wow, this doc also reminds me of that prior boss of mine—same demeaning tone and haughty body language.]

[Greta's Awareness: I'm going to have to be careful not to let my feelings get in the way here.]

Daniel (raising his eyebrows): "A leader?! Ha! I guess he is a leader of his surgical team, and does a fine job there; but I'd say he was a leader in name only when he got promoted to Chief Medical Officer. I do **not** appreciate working with Richard, so I'm having a hard time answering that question about strengths."

[Daniel's Annoyance: Richard is a good surgeon, but not a good leader. I certainly don't want to help him by listing any strengths.]

Even though Greta centered herself in advance, stakeholder Daniel is transmitting a variety of signals in his body language and tone that indicate he is resistant to this interview. The above example shows how it is not as effective for a coach to continue following the script of questions (repeating all the positive, strengths-based questions) without first acknowledging the powerful feelings a stakeholder is signaling through his tone and body language. Let's see what happens when Greta pauses to mention what she is observing.

Greta: "I see your eyebrows raised and hear some skepticism in your tone. What's going on for you in being asked to give feedback about Richard?"

Daniel: "OK, since you asked, I resent giving feedback about Richard. I think he's an arrogant know-it-all, not a team player, and he only got promoted because he runs a tight ship in the operating room! When he was promoted to Chief Medical Officer, it went to his head, and he ran meetings like we were his surgical team, with him the commander, dictating direction to us. He is **not** the boss of me or any of our colleagues. We resent his disrespect for us and our ideas."

[Daniel's Anger/Jealousy: It still burns me that he got promoted to Chief Medical Officer instead of me!]

[Daniel's Relief: Whew, it felt good to get that off my chest!]

Greta: "That's a lot of feedback. Usually I start by asking about strengths, but we can get back to that in a few minutes. Can we back up so I can get some specific examples from you about these conclusions you've reached about Richard?"

Daniel: "Sure, what do you want to know?"

Greta: "For example, when you said 'arrogant know-it-all,' what are some specific examples of Richard's behavior that led you to that opinion?"

Daniel: "That's easy. At our last meeting with the board, all department chairs were presenting. Richard looked down his nose at us over those reading glasses of his, and kept interrupting others' presentations as if he knew better than us what was going on in our areas. When he does that, he does not come across as a team player, but treats us like he treats subordinates. I don't know how that nurse Nancy puts up with that, but it's inappropriate for him to act that way with us who are his peers."

Greta: "What else?"

Daniel: "He also constantly checks his email and cell phone texts during meetings when others are presenting, as if what we are saying is not as important as him."

Greta: "Anything else?"

Daniel: "Yes, there is one more thing. He should stop interrupting Constance, who is our new department head of oncology; he interrupts her far more than the rest of us. She has great ideas, but he shoots them down with his criticism and focus on problems instead of solutions. She's told me she feels disrespected, and it's eroding her confidence. She also resents that Richard always allocates more resources for his surgical team than to other teams and doesn't value the other nonsurgical teams."

[Daniel's Excitement: Well, that should provide enough to make sure he doesn't become Chief Medical Officer again!]

[Daniel's Regret: Did I come on too strong? But it's all true...]

Greta: "Instead of that behavior, what would you prefer to see, hear, or notice in these meetings that would be more effective?"

Daniel: "Simple. Stop interrupting and start listening. Stop looking over those reading glasses and checking email and texts while others are talking. Give credit where credit is due."

Let's pause here. Clearly, Greta has her work cut out for her in terms of how to capture positive, actionable feedback from Richard's resentful colleague and understand what might be driving his perception of Richard's impact. It was important for her to be adaptable and improvise in her questioning once she noticed and sensed stakeholder Daniel's resistance to identifying anything positive about leader Richard. What emotions do you think Greta is experiencing that she needs to manage as coach? How could she elicit some positive feedback, and perhaps uncover the underlying emotions and impressions that drive the anger, from this individual stakeholder? What are some additional emotions or thoughts about Daniel that might be serving as "noise" to distract Greta from collecting the full spectrum of Daniel's signals?

Coach Question for Self: Avoid Being a Source of Distraction

☑ What is coming up for me? Am I setting aside whatever comes up and bringing an open mind to this interview?

☑ What am I noticing about this stakeholder? Am I being flexible enough in my questioning to make it safe for him to reveal valuable, actionable feedback in this interview?

C. Update Leader in the Interim

The final activity in Step 4 is to regularly update the leader between interviews. This is critical to strengthening the working alliance between coach and leader. While the coach is conducting interviews, the leader might be curious or anxious about progress. Be clear with the leader about when they can expect to meet to debrief the feedback report. Many leaders appreciate updates during the interview process, such as confirmation of scheduling and a brief overview of some interim high-level themes of initial feedback.

In the interim report or debrief, the coach might offer a positive comment that the leader would appreciate or a comment that the coach feels might buffer some of the suggested changes. For example, a coach might communicate to the leader that "people seem to be recognizing some key strengths" or "we are gathering some good specific examples for changes."

When the interviews are complete, encourage the leader to thank the stakeholders for offering feedback. This can take the form of a simple email or a handwritten note.

One Potential Pitfall: Organizations That Lack Direct Communication

A key to success when conducting stakeholder interviews is understanding the culture in which the leader operates and how communication is handled. If direct feedback is not valued within the culture or is avoided, the coach must be wary of unwittingly communicating feedback to the leader which the organization should have provided.

Among the pitfalls to avoid is being put in the position of "triangulating" between the stakeholder and the leader. What we mean by "triangulating" is delivering feedback the leader has never heard directly and which the coach should not be tasked with delivering for the first time. For example, if the leader's supervisor shares negative feedback with the coach that they have not shared directly with the leader, the coach is put into the awkward position of handling information that should have been delivered by the supervisor directly or through the organization's Human Resources function. Some suggested questions to ask if faced with this situation include:

- ▶ "Have you ever given this feedback directly? What's stopping you?"
- ▶ "What would it take to give that feedback directly to the leader?"
- ▶ "Would you be willing to meet and have a conversation with the leader and me?"

The coach must be wary of becoming the organization's outsourced communication provider and thereby feeding the organization's tendency to use triangulation instead of direct communication.

Just as what we focus on becomes our reality, what we fail to focus on creates a reality too. As this pitfall illustrates, sometimes a leader's reality is that their organization does not focus on the important role of feedback in professional development. Coaches can help leaders remedy this situation, yet in doing so must ensure that they are serving as the catalyst for feedback and not becoming a substitute for direct feedback. The coach can demonstrate the value of feedback and model constructive ways of obtaining and delivering it, thereby nurturing a more feedback-rich environment in organizations.

CHAPTER FIVE GUIDEPOST

It is important to:

▷ Create your stakeholder interview structure and use it as a guide, yet feel free to deviate from it as needed to meet stakeholders where they are and dig deeper.

▷ Bring an active listening mindset to the interviews and build trust as you ask interview questions and close the interview.

▷ Probe behind stakeholder judgments, biases, assumptions, and stereotypes about the leader to get to examples of the leader's actual behavior.

▷ Collect data (about behavior) as well as emotions and impressions, and the impact of the leader's behavior.

▷ Encourage feedback directly to the leader. Avoid delivering feedback the leader has never heard before from people within the organization.

▷ Keep the leader informed throughout the stakeholder interview process.

CHAPTER SIX
Stakeholder Feedback Framework Step 5:
Create Stakeholder Feedback Report

"What makes receiving feedback so hard? The process
strikes at the tension between two core human needs
—the need to learn and grow, and the need
to be accepted just the way you are."

—Sheila Heen and Douglas Stone, "Find the Coaching in Criticism"[11]

The interviews are complete, you have a collection of notes, and now is the time to create a feedback report that will best serve the leader in making changes. Sounds simple, right? However, as Heen and Stone recognize, delivering or receiving feedback is hard, given the tension between the leader's goals of professional growth and their human desire to be appreciated as they are. Recipients of feedback often take it as a critique of their person and performance rather than valuable information about their impact and needed improvement.

---

11 Stone and Heen, faculty members of the Harvard Negotiation Project, are also co-authors of the books *Difficult Conversations* and *Thanks for the Feedback: The Science and Art of Receiving Feedback Well* * *even when it is off base, unfair, poorly delivered, and, frankly, you're not in the mood.* While not written in the context of coaching engagements, both books are helpful resources for coaches seeking to structure feedback in a way that leaders can receive it well and learn from it.

Recognizing this challenge, the coach must build the report around what the leader needs to do to learn and grow, while acknowledging the leader's vulnerability and leveraging their strengths to accomplish that growth. This means that creating the feedback report requires so much more than just delivering data. Without attention to the leader's core human needs, as well as accurate capture and presentation of explicit feedback and implicit signals, the feedback report may be more disruptive than motivational to future change.

It is important that the feedback report be constructed with care because it is the codex for the full spectrum of stakeholder signals—their recollection of facts about the leader's behavior, their emotions and impressions, and their sense of the impact the leader has on them. In a sense, it functions as a mirror for the leader to look into, and they may not like what they see or may fixate on the negative rather than treating it like the developmental tool it's intended to be.

The report is created by the coach in three substeps:

STEP FIVE:

CREATE STAKEHOLDER FEEDBACK REPORT

A. Analyze the Data

B. Consider Reporting Preferences

C. Structure and Construct the Report

A. Analyze the Data

The coach must first analyze all the feedback they have gathered throughout the interviews, as well as remind themselves of the leader's development goals and preferences for how to receive information. Included in the data should be any insights the coach gleaned from observations about the emotions and impact resulting from the leader's behaviors. The purpose of the feedback report is to provide an accurate and actionable summary of the feedback from all the stakeholders. The coach must discern the dominant, recurring themes in the feedback and give priority to what is most relevant to the leader's development goals. The coach must also present the feedback in such a way that the leader is able to accept it and act on it.

In most cases, a descriptive, interpretive approach will be the preferred way to make sense of the data. To begin with this approach:

▶ start by reading the notes a few times, looking for common words or themes.

▶ look for behaviors mentioned by multiple stakeholders, both strengths and developmental areas.

▶ look for patterns and meaning across the interview notes.

▶ include specific examples.

▶ identify representative quotes.

Techniques that can aid the analysis include a simple tally system, color-coded highlighting, or word-cloud software. Be careful of accidentally losing anonymity (if agreed to) with feedback that could only have come from one source. The coach may occasionally need to go back to a stakeholder for help rewording an important piece of feedback to preserve anonymity or get permission to attribute an example. During your analysis, keep in mind the purpose for collecting the stakeholder feedback and the coaching engagement goals.

B. Consider Reporting Preferences

It's worth exploring the leader's preferences for oral or written feedback, as well as the content and length of the report. To craft an effective report, the coach needs to consider the leader's preferences for receiving feedback, including learning style, request for level of detail, the leader's relationship with feedback, and any concerns raised about the feedback process. The goal is to present the feedback in a manner that the leader can best receive and act on it. It is also helpful to align expectations regarding the report's level of specificity and use of explicit quotations.

Consider the feedback collected, identifying what will be easier or more difficult for the leader to hear. Where will representative quotes and examples be most helpful (within the agreed-upon confidentiality parameters)? Consider what you have learned about the system in which the leader operates. Is the organization a feedback-rich culture, where receiving and giving feedback happens often; or is this the first time the leader will have received candid feedback?

C. Structure and Construct the Report

There are several ways to structure the feedback report, depending on the leader's preferences, coaching goals, and context.

▶ **Themes and patterns structure:** Use the most prevalent themes and patterns as the headlines for the report, with specific behavioral examples and direct quotes (consistent with agreed-upon level of confidentiality).

▶ **Engagement goals structure:** Organize the feedback around the leader's goals for the coaching engagement.

▶ **Strengths-based structure:** Structure the feedback around the leader's strengths and how those strengths can be used to create desired behavior changes.

▶ **Development-based structure:** The report can be structured around the stakeholders' development suggestions, using behaviors to start, stop, and continue.

▶ **Interview questions structure:** It is also possible to use the structure of the interview questions themselves as the framework for the report, with a summary of each response.

These options are all viable. The best approach is one that is customized to meet your leader's needs and preferences.

We as Master Coaches pooled our knowledge and experience and shared the various feedback report templates we have used over the years. After doing so, we created a template that combines some of the most frequently used approaches.[12] In our template, we begin on the first page with identifying the leader's stated coaching goals and the intended focus of the feedback, and include a brief summary of all the strengths and of all the developmental areas. The following pages contain four major sections: specific strengths, specific areas of improvement, signs of future success (things to start, stop, and keep doing), and a reflection section (with a series of questions for the leader to complete after

---

12   See Appendix D, Sample Stakeholder Feedback Report, for sample feedback report. This example combines many of the structures suggested here for the coach to select what is most useful.

having gone over the report with the coach). Whether you choose to structure the report around themes or answers to the interview questions in each section is not as important as making sure that you include specific examples of actionable behavior that the feedback indicates the leader should continue or change.

One final note about timing required for this step in the process. Many coaches plan three to four hours to analyze the data, consider reporting preferences, and create a report with input from six to eight stakeholders. This timing assumes that the coach has developed and used a note-taking system that is efficient in capturing data that is to be included in the report. It is also important for the coach to discuss with the leader whether they want the report prior to the debrief or at the debrief coaching session. If the report is provided in advance of the debrief coaching session, it is wise not to provide it so far in advance that the leader has too much time to ruminate about any feedback that is less than positive.

Some Common Pitfalls

There are a number of potential pitfalls of committing to paper the data about your leader's behavior, emotions/impressions, and impact they have on others. Here are some tips for handling the most common ones.

Pitfall One: "Negative" Feedback

A commonly experienced pitfall is how to present "negative" feedback in a manner where the leader can take it in and learn from it. This problem arises when several stakeholders provide strongly negative or surprising feedback and the coach must decide how best to share the feedback in service of the leader's coaching goals. The coach must be mindful when presenting feedback so that it does not trigger the leader's defense mechanisms and/or powerful emotions in counterproductive ways.

Thus, the coach needs to carefully consider how to structure the report (and the debrief), so that the leader has the best opportunity to accept and engage constructively with difficult or unexpected feedback. The key is to write the report and unpack the feedback so it is least likely to set off identity and emotion triggers.

Some recommended strategies for reporting difficult feedback include the following:

▶ Begin with positive feedback, to set the overall tone of the debrief (while avoiding the disfavored "sandwich" critique, which buries negative feedback between two positive comments, thus obscuring it).

▶ Be specific: Provide concrete examples of behavior that can be changed.

▶ Be solutions-oriented: Give constructive comments and helpful examples that will suggest solutions.

▶ Be future-focused on actions: Highlight feedback on the leader's strengths that could be leveraged to change future behavior that is the subject of the difficult feedback.

▶ Be encouraging: Help leaders ascertain the significance of the feedback. Is this negative feedback career limiting, or a minor hiccup?

Pitfall Two: Outlier Stakeholder Comments

Another potential pitfall is presented when a provocative comment is made by only one stakeholder. Perhaps the outlier comment may even contradict the comments of other stakeholders, which makes it even more questionable in terms of its validity. Nonetheless, it is important for the coach to circle back with the individual to obtain more understanding of the stakeholder's perspective. Once deeper understanding is achieved, the coach must then carefully consider whether to report the one-off comment at all. Good practice would recommend not including sole comments in the feedback report or debrief, especially when they are contrary to all the other stakeholder feedback.

Pitfall Three: Coach's Own Preconceptions

Another pitfall to avoid in reporting stakeholder feedback is the potential for the coach to overstep the boundaries of their role as "curator" of the feedback and overly paraphrase, substituting their own perceptions about what is most important. While the coach must exercise discretion in the organization, themes, and tone of the report, this does not mean that the coach should inject their own views, values, and judgments to color the presentation of data in the report. Not only would that misrepresent the feedback, but it could be disempowering if the coach overinterprets patterns or implications, depriving the leader of the opportunity to make their own meaning from the data.

Specifically, the coach must be alert to the potential pitfall of misinterpreting the feedback patterns based on their own preconceptions or unconscious biases about the leader and about feedback. For example, sometimes a coach may have formed their own view of a leader's strengths and weaknesses based on a personality assessment tool, a past performance review, a demographic, or prior knowledge about other leaders in an organization, industry, or profession. The coach must be wary of letting their own views of the leader (or their organization or profession) drive how they present the feedback.

Pitfall Four: Coach reticence to present negative feedback

Another pitfall is presented for the coach who is uncomfortable with communicating negative feedback. This discomfort may cause the coach to sugarcoat or downplay difficult feedback based on the coach's own discomfort in relaying what may be perceived as criticism. If this difficult feedback is communicated by most of the stakeholders, the coach has an obligation to present it accurately, in a manner that the leader can receive and digest it.

The coach who struggles with this challenge would be well advised to request guidance as part of a coaching supervision group, and/or to hire a coach themselves to enhance their skills in delivering actionable feedback.

Coach Questions for Self: Creating the Feedback Report

☑ What have I learned and what assumptions might I be making after hearing all the feedback?

☑ Is something triggering a negative or positive perception? What do I need to do to manage self in this process as I write this report?

☑ How do I balance the leader's reporting desires with my perspective on the most effective structure?

☑ Am I honoring the agreed-upon confidentiality/anonymity terms with the creation of this report?

☑ Do I need to circle back with any of the stakeholders for further clarification?

☑ Is this feedback actionable, specific, and future-focused?

☑ How do I present this data in a way the client will hear it, especially if difficult?

☑ Have I determined whether the leader will receive the report in advance or at our debrief?

It is important to:

▷ Analyze the data and consider the leader's reporting preferences and development goals.

▷ Craft a report that effectively delivers actionable feedback utilizing themes, goals, and suggested future behavioral changes.

▷ Pay careful attention to the presentation of negative feedback so that the leader can accept and constructively engage with it.

▷ Avoid the pitfalls of creating a written feedback summary report by being mindful of my own preconceptions or any reticence to report negative feedback.

CHAPTER SEVEN
Stakeholder Feedback Framework Step 6: Conduct Leader Debrief

"Even if you get this feedback piece smooth and clear and perfect, with a set of perfect data, crystal-clear feelings, and well-defined impact all laid neatly on the table in front of you, you still haven't fully created the conditions for a learning conversation."

—Jennifer Garvey Berger and Keith Johnston, *Simple Habits for Complex Times*

Now it is time to debrief the feedback content with the leader in a way that creates the conditions for a learning conversation. As the quotation above brings out, even if the coach has done a great job in obtaining feedback and presenting it in a report, a key step remains: to deliver the feedback in a way that the leader can embrace it and learn from it. This is particularly true as most brains are wired to be "Velcro for negative experiences but Teflon for positive ones" (Hanson, 2018), leading to a tendency to ruminate on the negative. In sum, the overarching purpose of the debrief is to provide the leader with **actionable feedback, relating to their goals, in a manner that can be heard, accepted, and applied.** Thus, creating the safe conditions required for optimal learning is critical.

Please see the *Sample Feedback Debrief Structure* box on p. 162, which was created using the following five substeps:

STEP SIX:

CONDUCT LEADER DEBRIEF

A. Consider Timing of Report Delivery
B. Revisit Purpose of Stakeholder Input
C. Deliver Debrief with Emotional Safety
D. Gauge Leader's Reactions and Needs
E. Set the Stage for a Development Plan

A. Consider Timing of Report Delivery

The first important consideration for the debrief session is the timing of the delivery of the feedback report to the leader. Will the feedback report be sent in advance of the debrief or be shared at the debrief? Some leaders want to receive and review the report in advance in order to have time to process it. Others prefer to discuss the report with the coach and review it in further detail after the debrief. Consider timing the delivery to allow the leader to process the feedback, although not so early that they begin to spin their own commentary or develop unproductive concerns.

Breathing Life into It: Vignettes Regarding Timing of Report Delivery

In the following two vignettes, coach Greta demonstrates how the timing of report delivery can have a significant impact on the leader. In this case, the situation is exacerbated by the report content. Prior to this coaching session, Greta created an extremely detailed eight-page report that included every piece of information she gathered. She sent it to Sue several weeks before the appointment with no context, because she was very focused on "completely finishing this action item" on her long list of tasks for the week.

> **Greta:** "Sue, it's good to see you again now that you're back from your trip to the Grand Canyon. I hope you got the feedback report that I sent to you at your hotel."

> **Sue:** "My vacation to the Grand Canyon is a distant memory. Can we just get started with this report?"

[Sue's Anger: I am furious that Greta sent the feedback report to my vacation hotel! What a way to ruin my time off work.]

[Sue's Anger: I am mad at myself for ever agreeing to this.]

[Sue's Shame: Who has three pages of items to do better and gets promoted?]

Greta: "Okay, let's get started with the report. If we both turn to page 1, what struck you about your strengths?"

Sue: "Yes, yes, I read that. I wanted to go to page 4 and figure out what to do about all the weaknesses I apparently have!"

[Sue's Shame: I have so many things to improve, how will I ever measure up to these people?]

[Sue's Anxiety: Where does this put me and my career aspirations?]

Now let's look at how Greta might have set the stage for this debrief differently. In the following example, Greta honored Sue's preference for summary information and thought carefully about how much information to convey. She started the report with strengths so that these would not be overlooked, which often happens even in the best of circumstances. She also included some illustrative quotes throughout to help Sue see through her stakeholders' eyes. Sue received the report via email two days prior to the coaching session with a suggestion that she read through it and not overly analyze it. Sue was invited to ponder what she liked, what she was surprised by, and what she wanted to discuss in the session.

Greta: "Sue, it's good to see you again now that you're back from your trip to the Grand Canyon. When we last met, we had discussed today being the day we discuss your feedback report. How do you feel about doing that now?"

Sue: "The vacation was what I had imagined; I hiked and enjoyed the stunning scenery. I have read through my report and I am anxious to dive into it."

[Sue's Fear: I am worried about the negative feedback.]

[Sue's Joy: I did have some nice pleasant surprises.]

Greta: "What were some of your overall impressions?"

Sue: "I am truly valued for my business knowledge, beyond what I realized. I have a number of areas to work on that can help me, and I really want to discuss this."

[Sue's Joy: I think I can get some clarity from this session.]

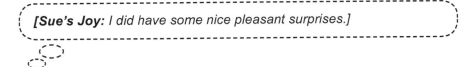

Coach Question for the Leader: Timing Receipt of the Report

☑ What's the best time for the leader to receive the feedback report: before we meet or when we meet?

Coach Questions for Self: Timing Delivery of the Report

☑ What do I know about the leader's style/preferences and the specific feedback in the report which may impact when I share the report?

☑ How can I meet the leader's preferences for summary versus details?

B. Revisit Purpose of Stakeholder Input

The debrief is a coaching session, not merely a download of interview themes or data. Thus, while delivering the debrief, the coach is well advised to revisit the leader's central goal for the engagement and focus the debrief on the feedback relevant to that central goal. For example, if a leader faces specific challenges related to creating a strategic plan and overseeing a transition, the goal of the debrief will be to identify feedback that indicates the leader's strengths and to focus on their development areas related to strategic thinking and change management. The goal of the feedback debrief should not be to cover every strength the leader possesses or every change the leader must make to be generally effective.

At the other end of the spectrum is the leader whose stakeholder input is being gathered toward the end of a coaching engagement. In this case, the coach will want to confirm that stakeholders have noticed progress on the leader's coaching goals and development areas. The feedback debrief should focus on areas of change identified at the outset of the coaching rather than explore in-depth new areas of opportunity (unless the coaching engagement has new goals).

As these examples illustrate, an appropriate plan for the debrief will depend on your leader's aims and preferences, as well as your own discernment about how to constructively convey the interview findings. Keep in mind that all the details will be included in the report, while the debrief is a coaching session that should focus on the areas most important to the leader receiving the feedback.

Coach Questions for Self: Prepare for Debrief with Goals in Mind

☑ How do I need to prepare for and show up with a mindset of coach—not just data deliverer?

☑ How can I connect to the overall coaching goal and not get too focused on what I learned in the interviews?

Coach Question for Leader: Check Preferences Based on Goals

☑ What will make our debrief discussion of the themes from the stakeholder interviews most helpful to you?

C. Deliver Debrief with Emotional Safety

Treat this time as a coaching session and a dialogue. Topics are likely to arise that need care and safety to be fully explored and understood. Stakeholder interviews are nuanced and personal, so must be treated with respect and curiosity. Think of the debrief coaching session as a sound studio that creates the optimal environment for the leader to hear the signals of change in an undistorted fashion, without any interference or static.

The leader will likely experience multiple emotions during the conversation—notice and discuss these. For example, the leader may feel excitement about others' confirmation of their strengths and development opportunities, or joy at having others notice their contributions. They may feel shame and the desire to linger on the negative themes or areas of weakness. Perhaps the leader will be surprised about a theme or criticism that is in their blind spot. Anger may show up if the feedback feels unfair, inaccurate, or critical of the leader's personality rather than of a behavior they can control or change. They may be concerned about sharing the feedback with their supervisor for fear their supervisor will lose confidence in them.

The coach has many roles in the debrief session. As mentioned, the first is to provide a safe place for the leader to feel free to explore their emotions as the feedback is revealed. The coach's role is both a mirror for the leader, showing the leader how others see them, and a light to explore perceptions, emotions, and stories. The coach is also a guide to help the leader sift through feedback, separating perception from fact. The debrief coaching session helps equip the leader to examine the facts behind the stakeholders' perceptions and identify the underlying behaviors at issue. The coach must create an emotionally safe environment for the leader to be able to hear and digest the feedback.

Sample Feedback Debrief Structure

No more than 90 minutes in length
Conducted in an environment conducive to privacy

1. Introduction and framing: identify the purpose of the debrief, the coach's role, and the level of confidentiality

2. (If you haven't provided the report in advance) Share the report and explain at a high level the layout and context for it

3. Ask the leader about overall impressions:
   - What resonates or is consistent with your experience?
   - What is pleasing? Surprising? Confusing? Disappointing?
   - What broad themes do you identify?
   - Have you ever had similar feedback?

4. Explore strengths
   - What does the feedback suggest are your key strengths?
   - What are some examples of you using these successfully?

5. Explore development areas
   - What does the feedback suggest are your potential opportunities for growth?
   - How much interest/energy do you have to work on these?
   - What might get in the way of making changes in these areas?

6. Wrap-up
   - What is your biggest takeaway or learning?
   - How will that make a difference?
   - Next steps to prepare for action planning?

7. Gauge reaction: ask leader what they need

Coach Questions for Self: Creating Emotional Safety

- ☑ How do I need to show up to bring emotional safety and honor our working alliance?
- ☑ What do I need to do during the debrief to keep the focus on what the leader needs and be present for him/her?
- ☑ How will I set aside any bias I have?
- ☑ Looking at the data: What is a fact rather than a perception?

Coach Question for Leader: Checking for Emotional Safety

- ☑ How does this feedback make you feel?

D. Gauge Leader's Reactions and Needs

Throughout the debrief coaching session, it is critical to gauge the leader's overall reaction to the feedback as it unfolds and explore their needs. As the debrief part of the session is concluded, invite clients to reflect on what they have learned in the session. Connect again to the leader's central coaching goals. For most of us, hearing feedback is deeply personal and can be difficult. The coach may be ready to move to action before the leader, or vice versa; be mindful of taking time to explore where the leader is and what they need next.

Coach Questions for Leader: Gauge Reactions and Needs

- ☑ What have you learned in our review of the interview themes (positives and things to change)?
- ☑ What is your single most important takeaway?
- ☑ How does the feedback connect to or clarify your coaching goal(s)?
- ☑ What do you need right now to continue to reflect on, absorb, and digest this feedback?

Coach Questions for Self: Exploring the Leader's Reactions and Needs

- ☑ How can I stay connected and pay close attention to the leader's body language and emotional reactions?
- ☑ How can I stay curious, letting the leader find his/her own takeaways?
- ☑ What pace does the leader need during this conversation?
- ☑ What do I know about myself that I need to manage? (For instance, a coach who likes action might move too quickly to discussing what to do as a result of the feedback.)

☑ If I am downplaying or sugarcoating negative feedback as a way to make the leader feel better, how can I counteract this tendency on my part?

☑ How have I helped the leader to focus on both strengths and gaps?

E. Set the Stage for a Development Plan

It is important, before the debrief coaching session is concluded, to set the stage for the creation of a development plan. The first step is to ask what the leader needs to process the feedback in order to take action in the future. The next step is for the coach to challenge the leader to come prepared at the next coaching session to identify two or three goals or action items as a follow-up to the debrief. Creating the development plan is discussed in the next chapter.

One consistent best practice is to separate the debrief of the feedback from the actual creation of a development action plan. This allows adequate time for the feedback to sink in before moving into action and development planning. Typically, the coaching session following the feedback debrief is the right time to commence tackling an action plan.

Breathing Life into It: Vignettes for Conducting Leader Debrief

Next, we will continue the leader feedback debriefing process where we left off before with coach Greta and leader Sue. In this next example,

Sue is still emotionally stressed from receiving her report while on vacation. She is preoccupied with discussing all the negative details. Greta works to restore her working alliance with Sue and reengage her coaching presence. Her earlier attempt to move Sue to a discussion of strengths was not successful, so she tries something else.

Greta: "Before we jump to page 4 of the report, let's keep in mind your coaching objectives:
  ▷ Growing your leadership overall;
  ▷ Focusing on stronger collaboration with your peers;
  ▷ Being seen as approachable and supportive of your direct reports; and
  ▷ Achieving a potential promotion to executive VP.
The goal of the stakeholder process was to shed some light on how best to approach these objectives. Is there anything else you want to add before we get started?"

Sue: [With some irritation] "I just want to jump into the report so we can discuss all of these areas for development you have listed here."

*[**Sue's Anger:** I don't know how they expect me to get all my work done without some strong words and energy to light a fire under these people. Yelling, huh?]*

[Sue's Shame: I know I can get excited and passionate; but having a temper, what is the matter with me?]

Greta: "What did you notice about this nice long list of strengths that your stakeholders see in you?"

[Greta's Shame: We are not in a good place. I have really screwed up.]

[Greta's Anxiety: I don't know if this will work, but I am going to try to move her into a positive space.]

Sue: "I read through them and I agree. But that doesn't tell me anything. [Pause] I work hard and know a lot about the business. If I am so great at these things, why haven't I been promoted yet?"

[Sue's Anger: It sure seems like they are expecting everything from me. I am known as the go-to person to get the hard stuff done. Then I get chastised for some yelling or strong demands. How in the world do they think these ridiculous targets can be met?]

[Sue's Shame: I am an impostor, not a top performer. What is wrong with me that I have four pages of weaknesses to work on?]

Greta has missed some important cues in Sue's tone and body language. Also, Greta's insistence on moving forward with Sue's strengths, without acknowledging Sue's obvious distress about the "weaknesses" described in the report, is interfering with their working alliance.

In this second example below, Greta begins with the good connection she is able to build with Sue early on in their feedback debrief coaching session. Although any stakeholder report debrief process between coach and leader is likely to spur both positive and negative emotions, Greta needs to avoid being drawn into Sue's tendency to become stuck in a negative, defensive place, while acknowledging the validity of Sue's emotions. Although Sue seems to want to move to the negative feedback, Greta needs to make sure she does not get drawn into the trap of too much focus on the negatives. Notice how Greta is more empathetic to and receptive of the signals Sue is emitting (while creating a more positive tone in the conversation).

> **Greta:** "I'll make sure we discuss your possible areas of improvement feedback in our session today, as I can see that is of great concern to you. Before we go there, I am curious to hear about a recent experience you have had with feedback that was positive for you. Can you think of one?"

Sue: "Well, a few weeks ago I was giving a presentation about a new consulting offering that I developed which I believe will be very profitable. I shared my ideas with the three Executive VPs. They were enthusiastic, but concerned our internal costs would be too high to achieve our profit margins. So I met with our CFO and demonstrated how the idea could meet our margin targets and add some great potential growth to the organization."

[Sue's Anxiety: I was unsure how to feel in the moment when I didn't get a resounding yes on the idea, as I am used to, and was nervous that the numbers would not pan out as I had promised.]

[Sue's Joy: I was glad they liked the idea, and the feedback really seemed to help me upgrade the proposal. There could be some value in this feedback thing.]

Greta: "I would like to add more context to your report and how it compares in general with other high-potential leaders. Would that be valuable to you?"

Sue: "Sure. Tell me more."

[Sue's Shame: I might not stack up well with other clients.]

[*Sue's Joy:* Greta would not bring up the comparison if it were not favorable in some way. I want to hear more.]

Greta: "Sue, many leaders find that receiving this kind of feedback can be a lot to take in, so please be gentle with yourself. Your results compare favorably to other high-performing executives. There is much strength to build on here. What strengths felt the best for you to read about?"

Sue: "Hmm, let me reread that section.
"I did like that people see me as hardworking. I've always prided myself on work ethic, and it's a strong value from my early years. I was pleasantly surprised to learn that I am seen as creative. I guess it is possible to be creative and an executor."

[*Sue's Shame:* I can't help glancing at the weaknesses, such as "needs to collaborate more." Priya is such an excellent collaborator. I never seem to hit the mark there. What will she think of me if I ask her help?]

[*Sue's Joy:* I do like some of these strengths.]

Greta: "Absolutely, it is possible to be an executor and creative! In your opinion, which of these strengths are most valued in your company?"

Sue: "Knowing the business and creatively engaging with the customers seem important to the CEO and executives. Understanding how the processes are executed and improved matters to my direct reports."

[Sue's Joy: I do have some important things going for me.]

Greta: "So how do you feel about hearing that creativity is a strength?"

Sue: "It feels good to be recognized."

Greta: "What else jumped out for you in your strengths?"

Sue: "I am smart and I am good with upper management."

Greta: "Is anything missing in your strengths that you wish was there?"

Sue: "Yes, I wish I saw something about collaboration, as that feels like the missing ingredient right now."

Greta: "How is all of this sitting with you right now? What do you need to process the feedback you heard?"

Sue: "I'm actually doing very well and want to talk about how I can get more collaborative."

Greta: "OK. Who is a great collaborator that you could learn from?"

Sue: "Well, that's easy—my boss, Priya Das!"

Greta: "What is a step you could take toward learning from her?"

Sue: "Since this is what Priya is all about, I probably just need to ask."

Greta: "Asking Priya Das is one thing you can do. Next session we can talk about other actions you can take as we construct your development plan. Here is a list of best practices for development plans. Would you be willing to look them over and think about what you want in your plan when we meet next?"

Learning from her other coaching sessions with Sue, Greta prepares differently for the debrief of feedback for Richard. This final vignette covers Greta's stakeholder debrief session with Richard, which starts off a little rocky, but ends on a high note.

Greta: "Richard, I understand you want today's session to focus on a debrief of the stakeholder feedback. Did you get a chance to review the Stakeholder Feedback Summary I sent a couple of days ago?"

Richard: "Yes!"

[*Richard's Discouragement: I can't believe that even my longtime friends find me intimidating and arrogant. This feels like a personal attack, not feedback.*]

[*Richard's Alarm: If I'm so terrible, how can I possibly become Chief Medical Officer?*]

Greta: "First, before we get into the specifics of the feedback, I want to just check in with you. I know that receiving feedback can sometimes be difficult. What was your overall reaction to the feedback?"

Richard: "I thought it was unfair and more of an attack on my personality. How can I change some of this stuff? Intimidating?! If I'm so intimidating, then how is it that my patients and team love me so much? I get rave reviews from them!"

*[**Richard's Defensiveness:** I wonder who said these things. If it was just Daniel, then I don't believe it; he's just out to get my Chief Medical Officer position.]*

Greta: "Feedback does sound personal sometimes. In the past have you ever received feedback that the impact you have is sometimes intimidating?"

Richard: "Well, that's what Jin Lei said in our meeting. And now that you ask, I guess I overheard that from one of my daughter's friends, when I was driving them somewhere after school. She leaned over to my daughter in the backseat and whispered 'Your dad is scary!' I don't want to be scary—that's not my intent."

*[**Richard's Regret:** I certainly don't intend to be intimidating...]*

*[**Richard's Anxiety:** What if I can't change?]*

Greta: "Ouch! That must hurt."

174

Richard: "Yes! So how can I change? I want to have a different impact than I'm apparently having right now."

*[**Richard's Hope:** If nothing else, perhaps this coaching and feedback could help me with my daughter, even if it doesn't help my colleagues to like me more and support me as their leader...]*

Greta: "I think your stakeholders have provided some specific behavioral examples of your strengths, which you can leverage, and your areas needing improvement. Keep in mind your overall coaching objective, which is not to change who you are as a person. Rather, as I heard your goals, they were focused on how to flex your interpersonal communications and leadership styles to more effectively motivate others to follow you."

Richard: "Yes, those are still my goals, and to become Chief Medical Officer again—don't forget that!"

Greta: "I haven't! What strengths did your stakeholders identify that you could leverage to make these changes in your leadership and communications styles?"

Richard: "Well, I like that they acknowledge I'm smart (so I can learn this stuff). And that they notice I'm empathetic with patients and supportive of my team. I guess I just don't feel as empathetic toward the other doctors and colleagues as I could."

Greta: "Ahh, that's an important point you made. You do feel empathy for some people and not for others. You asked earlier how you can change. Well, someone once said you can think your way into new behavior, or behave your way into new ways of thinking. Which comes easier to you?"

Richard: "I think I'm more of an action person rather than a reflective, navel-gazing kind of guy. I guess that makes you wonder why I became a doctor, eh?"

Greta: "Not at all. I see you as having strengths in both achieving and relating to others, especially with your patients and team, according to this feedback. Since you are an action guy, what behavior would you most like to change as identified in the feedback?"

Richard: "Two things. I clearly need to stop interrupting. And I want to change the way I talk so I come across as less intimidating, more open and respectful. I think if I stop peering over my reading glasses, checking my emails while others are talking, and focusing on my task list instead of really listening to others, that would help. I guess that's more than two things…"

[Richard's Anxiety: How can I accomplish all this? What if I fail?]

[Richard's Hope: On the other hand, what do I have to lose? Things apparently aren't working the way I've been approaching this leadership thing so far.]

Greta: "What's your key takeaway from this feedback that you'd like to focus on first?"

Richard: "Probably learning to listen more—that would stop the interrupting (as much) and my distraction with my cell phone in meetings. Hopefully, if I listen and pay attention to people more, I'll also come across as less intimidating, or 'arrogant.'"

*[**Richard's Shame/Humility:** I'm still hurt that people called me arrogant. But I suppose I do come across that way, as I am confident and I'm better than someone like Daniel. Perhaps I still have more to learn from others.]*

Greta: "Who is a great listener whom you could model, or connect with?"

Richard: "Actually, Constance, our new head of oncology, is a great listener. She's probably the one who said I interrupt too much. I could reach out to her and ask her for ongoing feedback during our meetings. And of course listen to her more."

*[**Richard's Appreciation:** I do admire how well she listens.]*

Greta: "Next session we can start work on identifying other actions you can take as you create your development plan. Here are a couple of templates of blank action plans so you can select the type that you think would work best for you. I'll then email you that template so you can start working on your plan. In our next coaching session, we'll continue creating that written action plan. How does that sound to you?"

Richard: "Fine. I just have one more concern. As I look at this template, I don't know what it looks like to write specific goals for all this 'soft stuff.' It's not like I can measure it, like 'fifty push-ups per day' as a fitness goal, or 'respond to all patient inquiries by COB' as in my patient care goals. What does an action plan look like when it comes to leadership?"

Greta: "Good question. You're not alone, as many leaders are challenged at articulating goals when it comes to leadership. First, start with your aspirational vision—what the end will look like. Then think of specific action steps to get there—resources to support you, books to read, people to reach out to for accountability or ongoing feedback, practices to begin to 'catch a habit in the act,' as they say. Does that help?"

*[**Greta's Anxiety/Regret:** There I go again, talking too much! Have I crossed the line from coach to consultant? How do I fight my urge to rescue this leader who struggles with articulating goals?]*

Richard: "I guess. I'm willing to give it a shot."

In the end, this feedback debrief resulted in Richard being able to truly receive the messages from his stakeholders and take them to heart. What are the questions Greta asked that helped catalyze this shift in Richard's thinking? How did she continue to build the working alliance between them? How would you assess her coaching presence?

In sum, the fundamental lesson regarding stakeholder feedback debriefs is to make sure you as coach treat this as a coaching session, and not as a delivery of the results from an assessment tool. Feedback is personal. It needs a personal, empathetic touch in order for the messages to be received and accepted.

CHAPTER SEVEN
GUIDEPOST

It is important to:

▷ Consider the leader's style, preference, needs, and views on feedback as you plan the leader debrief session.

▷ Carefully consider timing of debriefing the feedback report after the leader receives it.

▷ Review report with the leader, paying attention to and addressing the leader's emotional reactions.

▷ Remember this is a coaching session, not just a debrief of data.

▷ Don't get so focused on the themes from the stakeholder interviews that you lose sight of the broader coaching engagement goal. Connect what is learned from the stakeholders to the coaching goal.

▷ Bring a mindset of emotional safety and respect for the working alliance to the leader debrief session.

▷ Don't rush to decide what the leader needs to do as a result of the feedback; keep the debrief separate from creating the actions. Action planning is discussed in the next coaching session (and the next chapter!).

CHAPTER EIGHT
Stakeholder Feedback Framework Step 7: Co-create Development Plan[13]

"To create an inspired future, the purpose must become a dream, and the dream must become a plan. The dreamer becomes, in effect, a planner."

—Pamela McLean, *The Completely Revised Handbook of Coaching*

The step from feedback report to development plan requires courage, insight, planning, and even dreaming. It is the moment when the many discrete pulses of stakeholder signals converge and are transformed into one unified plan for the future. Creation of a written development plan is a valuable way for leaders to clarify their vision, goals, and action steps in order to achieve their objectives. Incorporating the insights from the feedback into the written development plan is a powerful way to process the feedback and to sift through what aspects of the feedback the leader chooses to act upon.

A development plan can be an iterative document that changes as the leader learns more from their experiments with behavior change (and possibly

---

13 See Appendix E, Sample Leadership Development Action Plan.

gains additional feedback). The development plan also provides a tool for the coach and leader to monitor the leader's progress and provide accountability.

Typically, the session after the coach debriefs the stakeholder feedback starts with discussing the leader's reactions to the feedback, moves to identifying what aspects of the feedback the leader would like to incorporate into their goals, and then ends with the co-creation of the action steps. If the feedback was difficult for the leader to hear, the coach and leader might spend more than one coaching session building the plan.

The coach should discuss with the leader what type of development plan would best serve them. There are many ways to build development plans, and leaders should consider their learning style and any relevant considerations regarding their organization's objectives.

While there are many ways to build the plan, the following substeps provide initial guidance on what to include:

STEP SEVEN:

CO-CREATE DEVELOPMENT PLAN

A. Begin with Vision and Aspirational Goals
B. Select a Few Focus Areas
C. Write Powerful Action Steps with Leader
D. Articulate Support, Obstacles, and Metrics

A. Begin with Vision and Aspirational Goals

The plan should begin with an aspirational vision of success. This vision acts as the "north star," motivating and guiding the leader forward. This overall vision is then made more concrete through articulating and prioritizing specific and measurable development goals. Throughout, the coach guides the leader in this reflection process.

Breathing Life into It: A Vignette for Beginning with Vision and Aspirational Goals

The following vignette illustrates coach Greta meeting with leader Sue to begin to co-create her development plan. Sue received her stakeholder feedback report and has had the opportunity to review it with Greta and to reflect on its contents. In turn, Greta has gauged Sue's reaction to the feedback; Sue is in a very open and receptive state of mind.

Greta: "Sue, it's great to see you today. When we last spoke, you indicated that you were ready to engage in creating some development goals for yourself based on the stakeholder feedback that we gathered. Is this still what you would like to focus on today?"

Sue: "Yes. I'm feeling very ready to do this today."

*[**Sue's Excitement:** I'm really eager to get some goals defined that I can begin to work on.]*

Greta: "Great! Let's start with the vision that you have and some aspirational goals. Based on the feedback that you've received and the reflection that you've done, what are some of the aspirations you have for your development?"

Sue: "I heard several themes in my feedback. Some of them were hard to hear. Things like my peers find it hard to work with me because they think I hog all the credit for work. You and I talked about how I think they mistake my passion and drive for wanting to be a 'ball hog.' Also, that my direct reports don't think I appreciate them and that I take them for granted."

*[**Sue's Shame:** I still feel like such a loser. I hate that I make people feel unappreciated and like it's all about me.]*

Greta: "I understand that some of that feedback was hard to hear. I applaud you for leaning into it. Now that we have the data, you have the opportunity to choose to do something with it. Ideally, how would you like to be perceived as a leader?"

[*Greta's Compassion:* She is hurting. I'm hopeful that she can use this data as fuel to feel better.]

[*Greta's Awareness:* Whoa, I'm noticing that I want her to "feel better." I need to manage my energy and avoid the tendency to "cheerlead" her here.]

Sue: "Hmm. I really like that question. (Pause) I'd like to be viewed as a leader who is strategic, who gets things done, who adds value to the business, and who has the respect of my boss, my peers, and my direct reports."

[*Sue's Hope:* Wow. That felt really good to say. I really do want to be seen as that kind of leader.]

Greta: "That's lovely, Sue. The vision you just painted is one I can see in my head and feel in my heart. I really like that you spoke not only about some of your opportunities to develop in your relationships with others, but you also highlighted some of your existing strengths: being strategic, getting things done, and having knowledge of and adding value to the business. How does it resonate with you?"

[*Greta's Joy:* I think she's on her path!]

Sue: "It feels really good to say that. I am committed to improving my relationships with others and to achieving my vision."

Greta: "Great. On a scale of 1 to 10, how committed are you to achieving your vision?"

Sue: "Nine. I want to achieve this!"

*[**Sue's Fortitude:** It will be hard work, but I'm committed to achieving this vision for myself.]*

Greta: "Wonderful. Our next step is to get clear about focus areas for your development plan."

Coach Questions for Self: Help Leader with Vision Statement and Aspirational Goals

☑ How can I challenge the leader to articulate a development vision that is both motivating and realistically achievable?

☑ What can I do to maintain an empathetic stance with a leader who is struggling to process painful aspects of the feedback without being a "cheerleader" or downplaying and sugarcoating things?

☑ How can I keep the leader in the driver's seat on setting their own vision rather than imposing my view based on what I ascertained from the feedback?

B. Select a Few Focus Areas

To start, help the leader pick a few critical areas on which to focus. It is often wise for leaders to limit the number of goals to no more than three at a time to focus and maximize their efforts. Then, explore the leader's aspirational vision for each area.

Coach Questions for Leader: Articulate Key Focus Areas

☑ Which aspects of the feedback resonate most?

☑ Which areas of feedback focus will provide the most benefit, or make the most difference, toward accomplishing your coaching goals?

☑ Where do you have the most energy to experiment and create change?

☑ What will be different if you create change in the areas you are considering?

Breathing Life into It: A Vignette for Selecting Focus Areas

Greta and Sue have engaged in a discussion about potential aspirational goals and have an understanding of what Sue's vision is for herself as a leader. The vision leverages existing strengths and considers some developmental needs. Now in this same conversation, Greta and Sue will take the vision deeper by identifying some specific focus areas.

Greta: "Sue, based on the vision you shared that you would 'like to be viewed as a leader who is strategic, who gets things done, who adds value to the business and who has the respect of my boss, my peers, and my direct reports,' what are some areas that you would like to focus on in your development work?"

[Greta's Excitement: I can't wait to see where she takes this!]

[Greta's Awareness: I need to be mindful about wanting change for her. This is her work to do, and I need to keep my wants out of the conversation.]

Sue: "I've thought about that. It seems like my biggest opportunities are to focus on building stronger relationships with my peers and with my direct reports."

[**Sue's Anxiety**: I worry about them being open to me reinventing my-self here. I hope I haven't burned bridges and that it's not too late.]

Greta: "What might stronger relationships look like with your peers and your direct reports?"

[**Greta's Self-judgment**: Darn. I should have asked about peers and direct reports one at a time. I know better than to layer my questions!]

Sue: "I'd like my peers to see me as someone who collaborates well, who gives them credit for the work that they do. I'd like for them to have great respect for me and my work, and I'd like for them to see me as a valued member of the team who is fun to work with."

[**Sue's Yearning**: I really want my peer relationships to be this strong.]

Greta: "Excellent. You seem to have a clear picture of what you want for your peer relationships. What do stronger relationships look like with your direct reports?"

[**Greta's Relief**: Now I get the chance to redirect and ask one question at a time. It's working out okay.]

Sue: "Well, I'd like my direct reports to see me as a strong and capable leader. I want them to trust me and to feel comfortable coming to me when they have ideas, questions, or concerns. I want them to know how much I appreciate them and respect them. And I want to know that they appreciate and respect me."

*[**Sue's Committed Desire**: I really want this. It kills me to think that this great team of people thinks that I don't appreciate them. They do amazing work, and I've got to find a way to let them know how valuable they are to me and to the organization.]*

Greta: "Again, Sue, you've painted a clear picture of what you want from your relationships with direct reports. I'm moved by your desire to let them know what they mean to you. It feels like that is coming from a very authentic place in you."

*[**Greta's Joy**: I'm so touched by her desire to connect with these people. This is what I love so much about the work that I do.]*

Greta: "Would you be comfortable moving these focus areas into action steps?"

Sue: "Absolutely."

*[**Sue's Optimism**: I'm ready to rock and roll!]*

Coach Questions for Self: Guide the Leader in Finding Focus Areas

☑ How can I assist the leader in breaking down their overall vision into a manageable number of development goals without being too directive?

☑ If the leader is stuck on negative feedback, which often happens given human negativity bias,[14] then how can I help them gain perspective on the bigger picture and focus on positive goals (e.g., "I want to do X," instead of "I don't want to do Y")?

☑ How can I help the leader tap into their excitement and motivation?

C. Write Powerful Action Steps with Leader

Remember that this is a coaching session with a goal of co-creating action steps to apply the stakeholder feedback. Once the leader has decided on the key focus areas, these areas should then be written as specific, step-by-step goals. Sometimes the coach may need to challenge the leader to make sure the goals are specific and actionable. For example, a stated goal of "become more collaborative" is not specific enough to be actionable—how would you know when this goal is accomplished? As the leader builds action steps, you and the leader might discuss the following questions.

---

14 Psychologists like Dr. Rick Hanson explain that the human brain has a negativity bias. Dr. Hanson describes the negativity bias as the tendency to focus on negative events rather than positive ones. He explains that we evolved over millions of years, dodging sticks and chasing carrots, and it was a lot more important to notice, react to, and remember sticks than it was for carrots (Hanson, 2009).

Coach Questions for Leader: Translate Goals into Action

- ☑ What will success look like when each goal is accomplished?
- ☑ What behaviors might be stopped, started, or adjusted to accomplish each goal?
- ☑ How do the leader's values, beliefs, and assumptions impact the goal?
- ☑ What mindset shifts, behavior changes, or new skills are required to accomplish these actions?
- ☑ What will make each action step manageable?
- ☑ When is it realistic to complete part or all of each step?

There are many templates for development plans and action plans.[15] Leaders can either choose an existing template or create their own. Consider: Is the plan only for the leader's use or do they intend to share it with others? The answer to this question may influence the layout and content to be included. Remember, leaders can be energized by starting with small changes. Incremental steps toward goal accomplishment will motivate larger efforts toward achieving the leader's desired future.

Considerations as you co-create the plan:

▶ For each development goal, the leader should identify the action steps necessary for progress. These action steps may involve the

---

15   See Appendix E: Sample Leadership Development Action Plan. This template is a compilation based on our experiences in coaching engagements. Coaches can pull from it what is most useful for them.

leader doing what could be described as "inner work" (reexamining values, beliefs, and assumptions) and "outer work" (acting or interacting in new ways). These steps may require mindset shifts, behavior changes, or the acquisition of new knowledge, skills, or practices.

▶ For ease of implementation, the action steps could include specific details about what the leader will continue doing, start doing, and stop doing. These steps should be small, manageable steps that are not too daunting to implement.

Breathing Life into It: A Vignette for Writing Powerful Action Steps

Greta and Sue have identified two focus areas for Sue's development plan. One is to build stronger, more collaborative relationships with her peers and the other is to build stronger and more appreciative relationships with her direct reports. Sue has articulated desired aspirational goals for each of these areas. While articulating aspirational goals is essential for motivation to make change, often those goals are not specific enough to be measured so that the leader knows when they've been successful. At this point, it is time to set clear targets within each of these focus areas and to make them actionable. These actionable steps are often coined SMART goals—Specific, Measurable, Attainable, Relevant, and Time-bound.[16] Greta and Sue continue the conversation to create these powerful action steps.

---

16 First coined by George T. Doran in a 1981 issue of *Management Review*, SMART criteria are also commonly associated with the work of Peter Drucker.

Greta: "Sue, our next step is to take the focus areas you identified to build strong relationships with peers and direct reports and to make those specific and actionable. In doing that, it can often be helpful to focus on how you might leverage your strengths as well. Let's give that some thought. What is your experience with setting specific goals?"

*[**Greta's Self-judgment:** Ugh. I did it again! I layered multiple thoughts into one statement to Sue. I'll be ready to clarify if I need to.]*

*[**Greta's Awareness:** I'd like to know what experience, background, and success she has had with specific goal-setting in the past.]*

Sue: "My experience with setting specific goals is pretty deep. Every year we set individual and team performance objectives using SMART criteria. Are you familiar with that?"

Greta: "Yes. I'm very familiar with SMART criteria in objective-setting. The definition I'm familiar with defines SMART as 'Specific, Measurable, Attainable, Relevant, and Time-bounded.' If you're comfortable with that model, we can use it as we establish specific actions. Would you like to use it?"

Sue: "Yes. That would be great."

*[**Sue's Relief:** Finally. We are working in territory that feels second nature to me! I'm great at setting specific goals.]*

Greta: "Great. Where would you like to start?"

Sue: "Let's start with my peers."

*[**Sue's Resolve:** I need their support to continue to grow myself as a leader and for Priya to consider me for promotion down the road. I've got to invest time and energy in these important relationships.]*

Greta: "OK. You identified your focus area here as wanting your peers to see you 'as someone who collaborates well, and who gives them credit for the work that they do.' You also indicate that you want 'them to have great respect for' you and for your 'work' and that you'd 'like for them to see (you) as a valued member of the team who is fun to work with.' Which one of those elements is the most important to you right now?"

*[**Greta's Awareness:** This is a big question. I need to give her some space and silence to ponder this.]*

Sue: (Pause) "I think a good place to start would be for me to start finding ways to give my peers credit for what they do."

[Sue's Awareness: This seems pretty easy too! I just need to look for ways to positively reinforce when I see something good happening with them.]

Greta: "That sounds like a great start. How might you do that?"

Sue: "Well, my boss Priya Das has a weekly staff meeting every Monday morning. I could take some time each Sunday night and think about a positive contribution that one of my peers made the previous week and mention it in the staff meeting."

Greta: "Yes. That's good. How might you think about recognizing peers that prefer more individual and private recognition?"

Sue: "Oh. That's a good point. I hadn't thought about that. I could send them an email message or stop by their office. Or, I could even invite them to lunch."

[Sue's Joy: I can do this! It might even be fun!]

Greta: "Great! How might you formulate that into a SMART objective?"

Sue: "How about something like 'Through year-end 2018, I will recognize one or more positive contributions by one of my peers at least once a week.'"

Greta: "Nicely done. My sense is that your setting this detailed SMART goal may prompt you to identify opportunities to recognize your peers that others may not see. Now let's identify an action you can take from your 'relationships with direct reports' focus area."

D. Articulate Support, Obstacles, and Metrics

The final step for the action plan is to discuss and write down what is needed to execute the plan. Identify the leader's support system and available resources. This means anticipating potential obstacles and corresponding proactive strategies. What does the leader know about themselves that might make leveraging the support system a challenge, and how can they mitigate challenges?

In order to ensure accountability, the plan should include some metrics for tracking the leader's progress. The coach helps the leader develop meaningful metrics by which progress will be measured. The coach and the leader should build regular review of the goals into their ongoing coaching engagement, iterating as needed. The leader may also assess their progress with their supervisor or another from their support system. Regular progress reviews can be motivating and can help garner additional support and feedback for the leader.

Breathing Life into It: A Vignette for Articulating Support, Obstacles, and Metrics

We now move into the final substep for Step 7. At this point, Greta is ready to assist Sue in articulating the support that she needs to implement her action plan, to identify any obstacles Sue may encounter, and to establish some appropriate metrics to measure effectiveness in realizing her goals for change.

Greta: "Sue, you've done some great work in establishing specific action steps to take to achieve your goals. Now let's talk about the resources you'll need to be successful. What support will you need from Priya Das or your peers in order to achieve your first goal?"

Sue: "I'll need Priya to know that I'm going to proactively recognize my peers when they do something well and make sure that she is comfortable with me doing that in various forums, including her staff meeting. I don't want her to get the impression that I'm trying to take over her meeting or usurp her leadership in some way."

Greta: "Excellent. So how will you get Priya's support for that?"

Sue: "I'll plan on asking for her support when you and I meet with her to review my development plan."

Greta: "That sounds great. Now let's talk about what might get in the way of you achieving your goal to recognize at least one peer, once a week for the rest of this year. Any thoughts about that?"

Sue: "When I get in my busy 'driver' mode, I can get very task-oriented and lose sight of some of the needs of others."

[Sue's Shame: Man, I hate that about myself.]

Greta: "Great self-awareness. How might you overcome that?"

Sue: "I'm not really sure."

Greta: "What kind of visual cue might you use to keep your awareness of others and the need to recognize them at a more heightened state?"

Sue: "What comes to mind is a Post-it note that says 'Who did something great today?' I could put it on my laptop so I see it throughout the day. It can remind me to make note of who did something that I can recognize with some good feedback and/or praise."

Greta: "Wonderful. I noticed the positive energy in your voice as you said that. You sounded excited to me."

Sue: "I was! I can't believe you noticed that!"

*[**Sue's Gratitude:** Wow. She is a really good coach. I'm lucky to have her. Maybe I should tell her that.]*

Greta: "It's great to see you in such a good place."

Sue: "Greta, you are a really good coach, and I just want you to know how grateful I am to be working with you. In the spirit of me noticing positive contributions to reinforce in others, I wanted to share that with you."

*[**Sue's Joy:** That felt really good to say. And look at Greta's smile. I think I made her day!]*

Greta: "Sue, I can't thank you enough for that. It has been my joy to work alongside you as your coach. I'm delighted that it has been valuable to you and I'm celebrating that just now you practiced with me exactly the type of recognition you want to use with your peers. Nicely done! Would you like to work on establishing a metric for this?"

Sue: "Yes, I would. I'm struggling a bit about what that might be."

Greta: "That's totally understandable. These kinds of things can seem hard to measure. What might be an indicator to you that your peers are feeling like you are sharing the credit for accomplishments and recognizing them?"

Sue: "Well, one might be that they thank me for the feedback and credit that I'm giving them. Another might be if I take the time to ask them periodically if they have examples of where I gave them credit for a job well done."

Greta: "Those are both excellent examples, Sue. I'll also offer that if at some point you would like me to do a quick one-question follow-up 'pulse survey' of your peers to see if they have examples of where your behavior has shifted, I would be glad to do that."

Sue: "That would be great. I can't wait to get started."

In the previous set of vignettes, Greta has taken Sue through each of the substeps in Step 7. Now we'll show Greta coaching Richard. We will show Richard without taking breaks in the vignettes in order to experience the arc of working with a leader who is resistant to development planning.

We begin after Greta and Richard have met to talk through the stakeholder feedback debrief. As you may recall from chapter 7, it was a conversation in which Richard expressed significant anger, emotion, and defensiveness. As a coach, Greta experienced the concept of "immediacy" with him and seemed to end the session on a positive note. (We define immediacy as noticing and commenting on a behavior or habit that is occurring in the present moment to build self-awareness.)

In this instance, Greta has already worked with Richard to identify a vision and aspirational goals as well as a first area of focus. We begin with Greta coaching Richard on how to write powerful action steps that will serve his learning (substep 7c). Let's see what happens as Greta attempts to assist Richard in bringing his development plan to life.

Greta: "Hello, Richard. How are you today?"

*[**Greta's Anxiety:** Well, let's test the waters and see what we're dealing with today. When we last met, he was really angry.]*

Richard: "I'm fine."

*[**Richard's Impatience:** Let's just get this thing over with so I can move on to my next patient.]*

Greta: "I'm glad to hear it. The last time we met, you indicated that you wanted to spend some time today to define specific actions you could take in your development plan. Is that still how you would like to use our time today?"

Richard: "I've already done my plan. Here it is." (Tosses a piece of paper to Greta.)

*[**Richard's Frustration:** I'm so done with this. Get me out of here.]*

Greta: "You worked on a plan. OK. Do you mind if I take a moment to look at it?"

*[**Greta's Fear:** Oh boy. What do we have here? Am I losing connection with this leader?]*

Richard: "Help yourself."

Greta: (Pauses to skim the paper) "I see that you have one action listed. It says you are going to have lunch with your boss, Jin Lei, once monthly for the next year. When we last met, you identified an area of focus that you wanted to pursue. It was 'learning to listen more' with the idea that it would help you to 'stop the interrupting (as much)' and it would help you with your 'distraction with my cell phone in meetings.' You went on to suggest that you thought if you 'listened and paid attention to people more, you'd also come across as less intimidating, or 'arrogant.' ... I'm wondering what happened to those items you raised when we last met?"

*[**Greta's Curiosity:** I'm sensing strong resistance here. I wonder what that is about?]*

Richard: "This is B.S. People are just jealous of me, and they are trying to hold me down. They know I'm a legitimate candidate for Chief Medical Officer and they're trying to torpedo me so that their chances are better than mine. I know what I need to do to get the job. I need to network with my boss and with the board members."

[Richard's Arrogance: I'm a major player around here, and everyone knows it. I'm the top-rated surgeon in this entire region of the country, and I have great administrative skills. I'd make an amazing Chief Medical Officer. I don't need everyone to love me. Just give me the job and I'll rock it!]

Greta: "I hear what you are saying, Richard. And, it is possible that some people may be jealous of you. I'd like to offer you another point of view to consider. Do you want to hear it?"

Richard (grudgingly): "Of course. Go ahead."

Greta: "As a coach, I have done hundreds, if not thousands of stakeholder interviews over the years. I'm trained to seek the most objective and actionable data possible for my leader clients, including you. I can assure you that the data that is summarized in the stakeholder feedback report came from multiple sources I interviewed, some of whom were not your peers and have no designs on competing with you for the Chief Medical Officer position. I'm sensing some resistance to this data from you, and I'm wondering what's causing it."

[Greta's Concern/Awareness: Now who sounds arrogant? I'd better watch myself here; once again he reminds me too much of that old boss of mine.]

Richard: "I'm not resisting anything! This is just idiotic—it's infuriating!"

[*Richard's Anger: Who does she think she is?*]

Greta: (Pause) "I'm sensing some real anger here. What's that about?"

Richard: "I'm angry that, after everything I've done for this hospital, anyone would tell me I'm intimidating, arrogant, and sometimes hard to work with."

Greta: "That sounds really hard to hear. (Pause) Sometimes when we experience strong feelings of anger, they are actually directed toward ourselves. What, if anything, might you be angry with yourself about here?"

[*Greta's Nervousness: I'm a bit nervous about going here with him, and yet I feel like I have a responsibility to hold up the mirror and show him what I'm seeing in service to his development.*]

Richard: (Pause) "I guess I'm angry at myself for letting things get to this point. All I've ever wanted professionally is to be Chief Medical Officer. And, now, because of some stupid behavior on my part, I feel that dream slipping through my fingers."

[*Richard's Distress: I'm a colossal jerk. How could I be so clueless about how others perceive me? Aren't I smart enough to know how to get people to like me?*]

Greta: "Right now, I'm experiencing you as deeply authentic and candid. I hear real longing from you about this Chief Medical Officer role. Given how important achieving that position is for you, how willing are you to make some changes that could position you for that role? On a scale of 1 to 10?"

Richard: "I guess I'm about a six."

Greta: "OK. What would make you an eight or even a ten?"

Richard: "If I knew that making these changes would give me the job, and not just be a waste of time."

Greta: "I hear you. When we spoke to Jin Lei, he indicated support and an openness to see you change and grow into the role. He also indicated that there are no guarantees. Given that, how willing are you to give it your best shot?"

Richard: (Long pause) "Well, it seems like if I don't try, I probably won't get the opportunity, will I?"

*[**Richard's Awareness:** If I don't take this seriously, I may regret it for the rest of my life.]*

Greta: "Given what Jin Lei said, likely not. What would you like to do?"

Richard: "I think I'd like to work on a plan that positions me to win the confidence of Jin Lei that I've overcome some of these perceptions of being arrogant and intimidating."

*[**Richard's Resolve:** Maybe I can overcome these perceptions. I'm going to do my best to try.]*

Greta: "I'm really glad to hear that, Richard. Shall we start with the focus areas you mentioned in our last coaching session?"

Richard: "Yes. That sounds good."

Greta: "OK. So, of the areas you referenced to focus on—'learning to listen more' (to help you to 'stop the interrupting as much'), working on your 'distraction with cell phone in meetings,' and coming across as 'less intimidating or arrogant' by listening and paying attention to people more—where would you like to start?"

Richard: "I think I'd like to focus on listening more, because I think it will help me become less intimidating to people."

Greta: "Great. What is your ideal state as it relates to listening to others?"

Richard: "I would like for people to see me as paying attention to them when they speak, and that they feel fully heard."

Greta: "That's lovely. I wonder if you have a sense of what gets in the way of you paying attention to people when they speak."

Richard: "I think it's my pace. I'm always running, and with a full schedule I don't have the luxury of a lot of time in-between commitments to chitchat with people."

Greta: "That's great awareness, Richard. One thought is that in our last session, you mentioned that Constance, the new head of oncology, is a great listener. You indicated that you thought you could reach out to her and ask her for ongoing feedback during meetings about how your communication is perceived. It could also be an opportunity to touch base with another busy doctor who may have some strengths in some of the informal hallway communication that came up in your feedback. She might be a good source for some suggestions as to how to recapture some of the margin in your schedule to make time for some of the impromptu conversations that may come up. What do you think?"

Richard: "I really like that idea. I'm going to set up a meeting with her when I get back to the office today."

Greta: "Sounds like a good first step. You also indicated that you have some interest in better self-management as it relates to checking your cell phone in meetings. Would you like to explore that?"

Richard: "Yes."

Greta: "OK. I invite you to take a minute and picture yourself in a meeting. When you reach for your cell phone, what is the first impulse you feel before you reach for it?"

Richard: "It's either 'What am I missing?' or 'I'm bored in this meeting.'"

Greta: "OK, great awareness. Which one of those happens with the most frequency?"

Richard: "It's definitely the 'I'm bored in this meeting.'"

Greta: "OK. And by reaching for your cell phone, what is the message that you think you're delivering to people?"

Richard: "Hmm, that I'm not interested in what they are saying."

Greta: "So if you seem disinterested, do you see a link between that and the perception of arrogance?"

Richard: "Yes. I guess I seem a bit self-involved."

Greta: "How would you like to be perceived?"

Richard: "As attentive, listening well, and more humble than I am now."

[*Richard's Pride*: I like the sound of that.]

Greta: "Well-said. What is another choice you could make in the meeting that would allow you to be more engaged and to show up in a way that is attentive, listening well, and more humble?"

Richard: (Pause) "I could take notes on the meeting. I could also ask questions in the meeting to show my interest in a topic. Or, maybe I could even compliment someone on their ideas or their work."

Greta: "Excellent. How might you give yourself a cue when you are tempted to reach for your cell phone?"

Richard: "I saw a motivational phrase on a colleague's cell phone wallpaper. It read 'You can do anything!' I'm going to put that on my cell phone so that it's the first thing I see when I look at it. It will remind me that I can do this if I want to be Chief Medical Officer badly enough."

[Richard's Excitement: I really think I can do this.]

Greta: "Wonderful. We're nearly at the end of our time today. You've done some amazing work. Would you be comfortable taking another shot at writing your development plan given this conversation and sending it to me? We can then use that draft to finalize the work in our next session."

Richard: "That sounds good. I can do that."

Greta: "Super. I look forward to seeing your revised plan and to seeing you in two weeks."

[Greta's optimism: I think he's on his way to making some great changes for himself.]

What Greta experienced with Richard is not that uncommon when coaching leaders who come into coaching reluctantly. In those instances, there might be a tendency to reject any negative comments in the feedback and to resist writing down any specific changes (for fear it would be admitting others were "right" and they were "wrong"). As the preceding vignette demonstrates, it is a delicate balance to challenge the leader while preserving the working alliance essential to the coaching relationship.

Coach Questions for Self: Support the Leader in the Development Plan

☑ How can I manage my own feelings and triggers when the leader expresses emotional responses to incorporating feedback into action steps?

☑ How can I challenge the leader to explore ideas about new behaviors that take them out of their comfort zone while still being supportive and maintaining a strong working alliance?

☑ How do I meet the leader where they are? For example, how do I meet their fear of change or the pace of change by helping them focus on small, manageable steps forward?

Finally, when the development plan is completed, the leader and coach should consider whether there are any stakeholders with whom the leader would like to share their development goals. There may be situations where sharing portions of the plan would be a positive gesture to stakeholders and allow them to support the leader's development goals.

CHAPTER EIGHT GUIDEPOST

It is important to:

▷ Help the leader focus on creating a motivational but realistic vision, goals, and action steps that incorporate the insights from feedback to guide their development.

▷ Guide the leader to focus on a few important development areas and set positive goals.

▷ Keep the leader in the driver's seat regarding what aspects of the feedback they want to act on.

▷ Assist the leader in coming to terms with negative feedback and difficult emotions related to that feedback without "cheerleading," downplaying, or fixing.

▷ Manage the coach's own feelings about the leader's emotional reactions to feedback.

▷ Support the leader in taking on their development challenges while helping them focus on manageable steps forward.

CODA
From Signal Flame to Full Illumination

"Yesterday I was clever, so I wanted to change the world.
Today I am wise, so I am changing myself."

—Rumi

This is the final guidepost on our journey. It requires wisdom and versatility to follow, because it points both outward, to the future, and inward, to a changing self. It is much like the signpost a hiker encounters on a steep stretch of trail which reveals that the distance to the summit is longer and the path less clear than expected. To approach the summit requires not only following the signs, but also improvising our steps, fortifying our inner resolve, transforming our mindset, and persevering when our strength fails us.

We are honored to have served as your guides and happy to have lit the way, one small but focused flame after another, through each step in the Stakeholder Feedback Framework. We hope you will use the framework to seek transformation—in yourselves as coaches and in the leaders whom you coach. The templates, best practices, and application ideas that accompany the framework are meant to help you develop your own techniques for bringing the right mindset and questions to every leadership coaching engagement.

As you continue your journey in applying the framework, questions will likely arise. What does it look like to have a strong working alliance with the leaders you coach, and how does the stakeholder feedback process deepen that alliance? What does it mean to be mindful of your coaching presence in every step of the feedback process? How can you remind yourself, in the moment, to be fully present—to your own emotions, those of the leader or stakeholder, and to the environment of the organization?

Our hope is that our work will help you answer these questions so that you can improve the process of seeking and accepting feedback in leadership coaching and transform it into more than a one-time exercise. We hope our guidebook will inspire a broader view of feedback, not as a static event, but as an ongoing, integral part of a richer culture of two-way communication. In this type of culture, leaders and organizations would seek and use feedback regularly in the service of leadership development.

There is a different pathway for each party in this ongoing process. Coaches, leaders, stakeholders, and organizations will experience different kinds of transformation in embracing the iterative process of the framework. Coaches who become masterful in the full process of gathering and delivering feedback will serve as excellent role models of how to listen well, manage their feelings, observe emotional signals, and be resilient when things get off track. Coach and leader can bring to the feedback process a new self-awareness, strong working alliance, and sense of the leader's purpose. Ultimately, the coach's role will be to help the leader integrate feedback into their own unique developmental learning agenda, cultivating rich soil for exponential leader growth.

Leaders will also be transformed as a result of a successfully conducted stakeholder feedback process. In addition to catalyzing greater self-awareness in the leader, an effective feedback process has the power to create stronger relationships between leaders and their stakeholders so that stakeholders become a support system for change. For example, a stakeholder can support a leader's change efforts by actively recognizing the leader's efforts to experiment with new behaviors and alerting the leader when their undesired old behavior patterns reappear. This is the type of ongoing systemic support that allows leaders to reach their development goals.

While pointing to the future, this book is also retrospective—we are fervent advocates for this framework because we have experienced firsthand the importance of trust, openness, and deep listening in the stakeholder feedback process. In essence, we were travelers before we were guides.

You might wonder how we, and the leaders whom we coached, were shaped by our journey of creating and fully integrating the framework into our coaching engagements. What is the view from further along the path? The following are a few stories of how we were impacted as coaches and the impact we saw in the leaders whom we coached.

Snapshots from Further Along the Path

▶ *I am a better coach to my clients because of the learning experience of receiving and delivering stakeholder feedback as part of the Master Coach Program. This, along with the process of codifying our learning through the writing of this book, has given me more empathy and awareness of the vulnerability around stakeholder feedback. I make fewer assumptions and ask more check-in questions of clients.*

▶ *After a stakeholder feedback process with my client, she spoke of the power of understanding how she is perceived by others. While some of the feedback was hard to hear and took time to experiment with and to integrate changes, she spoke of the gratitude she has for her stakeholders and the coaching process.*

▶ *One of the leaders I coached was very motivated to change her leadership approach, but prior to the coaching and stakeholder feedback, she could not put her finger on why she had not made the progress she desired. Her stakeholder feedback provided specific examples of what others saw her doing and not doing that impacted her effectiveness as a leader. The manner in which the leader requested help from her stakeholders, and shared her vision and how the feedback fit into that vision, made a substantial difference in motivating the shareholders to be open. Based on our very strong working alliance, she was able to hear the feedback and recognize a fundamental assumption she had been making that was getting in her way.*

▶ *I'm a lot better at gathering and delivering stakeholder feedback as a result of writing this book, creating this framework, and enacting some of these vignettes onstage (and expanding upon them in this book). I used to treat some aspects of stakeholder feedback in a rather perfunctory manner. I wasn't really in tune with how the emotions are woven into every step of the process. That has now changed.*

▶ *Many leaders whom I coach have indicated the stakeholder feedback was the most valuable tool in the coaching, because it provided specific information about how they could be more effective. For example, one leader initially was very resistant to feedback because in past 360-degree, anonymously written performance evaluations, he felt attacked, with no means of defense or ideas for how to change. Through our stakeholder feedback process, he discovered actionable behavior and ways to discern the difference between data, emotions, and impact to identify specific changes he could make. Incredibly, a year later, he even approached me to embark on a new stakeholder feedback process to discern what progress he's made.*

▶ *For me, this path has been a rich one, with many peaks and valleys. I feel more empathetic as a coach, more sensitized to the emotional climate (and triggers) of the leaders I coach, and more aware of the signals the organization is transmitting when I am navigating through a stakeholder feedback process. I realized along the way what a critical role the coach plays in transforming what is often evaluative feedback focused on the past (which cannot be changed anyway) into future-facing solutions and optional avenues for change. The key is to elicit specific examples of recommended future behavior and precise actions a leader could take for greater effectiveness. This very act can transform judgmental feedback into empowering options for future change.*

Creating this framework, being mindful at every step, and writing the vignettes for this book has made the stakeholder feedback process come alive for all of us. We are more curious and more empathetic about how vulnerable many of our client-leaders feel about each step of the process, and we know firsthand the benefits of stakeholder feedback in promoting a leader's professional growth. We hope we have communicated what we have learned about the importance of understanding and addressing the emotional challenges that can arise in the process for the leader, the coach, and the stakeholders. We hope we have elicited moments of recognition (and perhaps even knowing laughter) in the emotional moments played out in the vignettes. Lastly, we hope that the many connections and exchanges made during each step of the Stakeholder Feedback Framework will illuminate a pathway to real change for every person or organization that participates in the process.

ACKNOWLEDGMENTS

We owe a debt of gratitude to several people who were instrumental in our growth along the journey. The first is Pam McLean. As co-founder of the Hudson Institute of Coaching, Pam has made an indelible imprint on the coaching industry and on each of us as Graduate Master Coaches. Pam: We thank you for your clear vision, for your remarkable insight, and for your groundbreaking mastery. You serve as such a beautiful model of lifelong learning for coaches and organizations, showing how to continuously find new approaches for the betterment of our world.

We also offer our deepest thanks to Sandy Smith. As a valued member of the Hudson Faculty for the last fifteen years, Sandy is an inspiration to the Hudson Coaching Community. San: We thank you for your generosity of spirit and time, and for offering your selfless and helpful feedback to us in the service of our self-development and continuous growth. We are all better for it! Your ongoing sharing of your expertise in stakeholder feedback, including in the Master Coach Program, was a real catalyst for this work.

We also offer our profound thanks to Doug Silsbee, Master Somatic Coach and guest faculty in our Master Coach Program along with Pam and Sandy. Doug's humble, safe, and open heart served as a blank canvas from which he taught as gentle and wise guru of somatic coaching and foundational insight. It was a privilege and joy learning from him, and it is with heavy hearts we acknowledge his recent passing. We have each been changed by Doug's transformational work with us in the Master Coach Program. We hope to honor Doug's legacy as we lean into the power of this book.

We would like to acknowledge our fellow travelers along the 2016 Master Coach Program Journey. Leslie Goldenberg, we thank you for your many contributions to the early part of this writing, including significant contributions to the literature review. To our other classmates: Deb Gerardi, Russ Hall, Cindy Levine, Rafael Pacchiano, we are grateful for the generous feedback you've shared, for your willingness to learn with us as we experienced our own stakeholder feedback, but most of all for your continued friendship.

We can't imagine this labor of love, toiled over for twenty-two months by our team of seven master coaches, being what it is today without the guidance and professional expertise of Nathinee Chen and Bethany Kelly.

Lastly, we are grateful to all of our coaching clients, who trust us to walk alongside them on their leadership journeys, including sometimes challenging conversations about feedback.

We are honored to have each of you in our lives.

FREE DOWNLOADS!

Visit our book's website to download resources and save time: www.fearlessfeedbackguide.com

Resources include free downloads of

- ▶ Seven-step Stakeholder Feedback Framework
- ▶ Templates:
  - ▷ Sample leader email to stakeholders requesting interview
  - ▷ Sample stakeholder questions
  - ▷ Sample stakeholder feedback report
  - ▷ Sample leadership development action plan

FEARLESS FEEDBACK

APPENDIX
Introduction

This appendix contains sample forms and the more detailed model of the Feedback Framework to help readers with the stakeholder feedback process described in the guidebook. These samples include a number of topics and options, and are intended as a starting point for discussion. Readers are welcome to customize templates as they wish.

Appendix A: Stakeholder Feedback Framework with Substeps

Visit www.fearlessfeedbackguide.com to download the full-color framework.

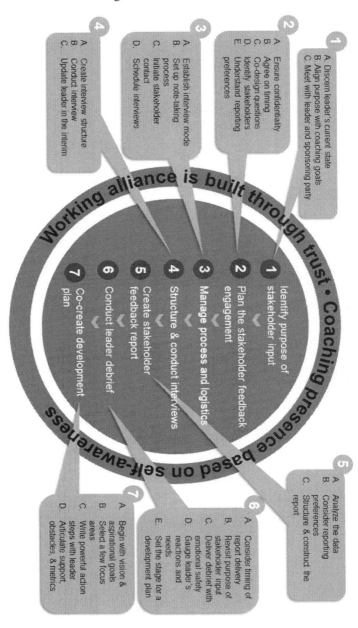

1
A. Discern leader's current state
B. Align purpose with coaching goals
C. Meet with leader and sponsoring party

2
A. Ensure confidentiality
B. Agree on timing
C. Co-design questions
D. Identify stakeholders
E. Understand reporting preferences

3
A. Establish interview mode
B. Set up note-taking process
C. Initiate stakeholder contact
D. Schedule interviews

4
A. Create interview structure
B. Conduct interview
C. Update leader in the interim

5
A. Analyze the data
B. Consider reporting preferences
C. Structure & construct the report

6
A. Consider timing of report delivery
B. Revisit purpose of stakeholder input
C. Deliver debrief with emotional safety
D. Gauge leader's reactions and needs
E. Set the stage for a development plan

7
A. Begin with vision & aspirational goals
B. Select a few focus areas
C. Write powerful action steps with leader
D. Articulate support, obstacles, & metrics

Working alliance is built through trust • Coaching presence based on self-awareness

1 Identify purpose of stakeholder input
2 Plan the stakeholder feedback engagement
3 Manage process and logistics
4 Structure & conduct interviews
5 Create stakeholder feedback report
6 Conduct leader debrief
7 Co-create development plan

Appendix B:
Template of Leader Email to Stakeholders Requesting Interview

Time-saving download at www.fearlessfeedbackguide.com

Dear _____,

As you know, I have recently begun working with an executive coach, who is gathering feedback to inform my professional development. As you and I discussed, I am requesting your participation in the stakeholder feedback collection process that my coach [coach name], (a certified leadership development coach), will be conducting.

I would appreciate it if you'd be willing to participate in a ____ [insert duration in minutes] meeting or phone interview with [coach name] where [he/she] will seek your input.

I welcome your candid feedback. The interview [or specific parts of the interview] will be confidential [specify how confidentiality will be handled; see guidebook, chapter 3, section A regarding options for handling confidentiality]. My coach will provide me with a summary of the feedback. [Can specify whether the summary will include key themes, comments and/or quotations, with or without specifying the source of particular feedback, depending on how confidentiality is handled].

Many thanks for your willingness to participate, and for taking the time to speak with [coach name]. I have copied them on this email so they can reach out to you directly [during X timeframe] to schedule a time for the interview. If you have any questions, please let us know. Thanks again.

All the best,

_____

Appendix C: Template of Sample Stakeholder Questions

Time-saving download at www.fearlessfeedbackguide.com

Feedback for: _____

Feedback from: _____

Date: _____

Note: This list of questions covers several typical feedback topics. We expect that the coach and the leader will customize by choosing the most relevant questions and limiting the number of questions to fit the time allotted for the interview.

Questions:

1. How long have you worked with [*name*] and in what contexts?
2. Describe [*name's*] top strengths in performing their role and/or what you appreciate about [*name*]:
   a. Provide examples of these strengths in action based on your observations
   b. How can s/he leverage these strengths to improve performance?
3. Describe [*name's*] challenges and a couple of adjustments s/he could make to be more effective:
   a. Provide examples illustrating these challenges and how s/he could have handled things better
   b. What gets in the way of [*name*] being most effective?
4. [*name's*] development goals are to: [*list goals*]. How do his/her strengths and areas for improvement relate to these goals?

5. What are 1–2 suggestions for [*name's*] success in the future to be even more effective? What specific actions could s/he take?

   a. Keep doing or continue to improve on?

   b. Start doing?

   c. Stop doing?

6. What are the key qualities or abilities s/he needs to develop to become a great [*insert target role: for example, leader, manager*]?

7. Do you have any other comments or suggestions for [*name*]?

8. If [*name*] wanted your help in providing feedback along the way, would you be willing?

Appendix D: Sample Stakeholder Feedback Report

Time-saving download at www.fearlessfeedbackguide.com

SECTION 1—SUMMARY

Summary of confidential interviews conducted between	Number of people interviewed:
_____ _____ Begin date End date	

Leader's coaching goal(s) and the focus or purpose of the feedback

Any insight or feedback about the process which stakeholders shared

Overall summary of what was shared (patterns and/or themes)

Overall areas of strengths

Overall areas of possible adjustments/opportunities

Other

SECTION 2—KEY STRENGTHS

What are [name's] top strengths when s/he is working at [his/her] best?

List the specific positive/appreciated attributes shared that tie to the focus of feedback

Provide explicit behavioral examples from the interviews of strengths in action

_____   _____

_____   _____

_____   _____

SECTION 3—KEY DEVELOPMENT AREAS FOR FUTURE SUCCESS OR GREATER EFFECTIVENESS

What could [name] start doing, stop doing, or continue to improve upon?

List specific comments received during the interviews about possible areas of growth or change

Give constructive examples shared of behavior or changes that would be appreciated

_____   _____

_____   _____

_____   _____

SECTION 4—ADDITIONAL COMMENTS

List any additional insights shared

SECTION 5—REFLECTION QUESTIONS FOR [NAME]

[NOTE: Next section to be left blank, and completed by leader after processing above feedback.]

Reflect on the above feedback, and process feelings evoked by it; put it in perspective

Identify what stands out for you: what you know and any surprises, positive and negative

Determine what aspects of feedback you want to take on

What are the most important insights/takeaways

Decide what feedback will be shared with others

If shared with others, think about who, when, and where

Appendix E: Sample Leadership Development Action Plan

Time-saving download at www.fearlessfeedbackguide.com

LEADERSHIP DEVELOPMENT ACTION PLAN (based on stakeholder feedback) (Identify what aspects of the feedback were most useful/resonated that you want to capture and act on below)	
Strengths (keep doing) (Describe stakeholder feedback which speaks to your strengths and what you want to keep doing)	**Areas of Opportunity (start doing/stop doing)** (Reflect on the feedback about growth opportunities; then identify what you want to start or stop doing for ongoing development)

Aspirational Vision (desired future)	Accomplishments to Date (List those which reinforce skills & potential)	What Are You Passionate About?

Short-term Development Plan (High-level list of actions to consider taking, including behavioral changes, mindset shifts, skill acquisition or refinement)	Obstacles (Identify what might get in the way of accomplishing your goals. Reflect: What's going to make this development plan hard to do?)

Specific Short-Term Development Goals	Impact of Achievement	Actions to Take (SMART goals) (Specific, Measurable, Attainable, Relevant, and Time-bound)	Resources/Support Required (List resources needed: people, systems, processes, books, models, money, etc.)
Goal 1			
Goal 2			
Goal 3			

REFERENCES

Bariso, Justin. (2018). *EQ applied: The real-world guide to emotional intelligence*. Germany: Borough Hall.

Batista, Ed. (2013, December). Building a feedback-rich culture. *Harvard Business Review*. Retrieved from https://hbr.org/2013/12/building-a-feedback-rich-culture.

Flaum, J. P. (2010). *When it comes to business leadership, nice guys finish first* (A study from Green Peak Partners and Cornell's School of Industrial and Labor Relations). Retrieved from http://greenpeakpartners.com/uploads/Green-Peak_Cornell-University-Study_What-predicts-success.pdf.

Garvey Berger, Jennifer, & Johnston, Keith. (2015). *Simple habits for complex times: Powerful practices for leaders*. Stanford: Stanford University Press.

Hammond, Sue Annis. (1998). *The thin book of appreciative inquiry* (2nd ed.). Bend, OR: Thin Book Publishing Co.

Hanson, Rick. (2009). *Buddha's brain: The practical neuroscience of happiness, love, and wisdom*. Oakland, CA: New Harbinger Publications.

Hanson, Rick. (2010, October). Stephen Colbert: We don't need to "keep fear alive" [blog post]. Retrieved from https://www.rickhanson.net/stephen-colbert-we-dont-need-to-keep-fear-alive/

McLean, Pamela. (2012). *The completely revised handbook of coaching: A developmental approach.* San Francisco: John Wiley & Sons.

Silsbee, Doug. (2008). *Presence-based coaching: Cultivating self-generative leaders through mind, body and heart.* San Francisco: Jossey-Bass.

Stone, Douglas, and Heen, Sheila. (2014). *Thanks for the feedback: The science and art of receiving feedback well.* New York: Penguin.

ABOUT THE AUTHORS

REBECCA GLENN

Rebecca Glenn is the owner of TOP Coaching and Consulting LLC www.topcandc. com, where TOP stands for Tenacity of Purpose. She has been coaching leaders and teams at all levels for over 10 of her 30+ years of professional business experience. Offering a wealth of insight from her diverse leadership roles, she relates to the difficulties leaders face. Clients appreciate her empathy and grasp of their situations. She is passionate about helping clients create sustainable habits and techniques for success, teamwork, and happiness.

Rebecca's varied experience includes roles as Executive Coach, Business Owner, VP/Chief Information Officer for ON Semiconductor,

VP of Technology for Nautilus Insurance, Nonprofit Co-Founder, and other key leadership roles for Motorola and Accenture Consulting.

She has deep expertise in Emotional Intelligence, Qualitative 360 reviews for Leaders, Leadership, Program Management, Change Management, Innovation, and High-Performance Work Teams.

Rebecca has a Bachelor of Science degree in Quantitative Business Analysis from Arizona State University, graduating *summa cum laude*. She is a Hudson Institute Master Coach, Professional Certified Coach through the International Coach Federation, and is certified or trained in numerous tools such as EQ in Action, Myers-Briggs Type Indicator, DiSC and Design Thinking.

Rebecca is a native Arizonian, located in Phoenix, married with two adult children and part of a large extended family. She is an outdoor person, and three of her favorite hobbies are skiing, hiking, and scuba diving. She is lucky to be able to do the work that brings her alive—having conversations that matter and helping others create their best future.

You can reach her at Rebecca@topcandc.com or linkedin.com/in/reglenn.

PENNY HANDSCOMB

Penny Handscomb has lived and worked in the US, Canada, Israel, UK, and spent a significant amount of time in emerging markets, where she has helped build businesses with a main focus on human capital. She has spent a great deal of time helping organizations scale as well as manage change. Penny is a master coach, board member, and past adjunct professor.

More specifically, for the past nearly four years Penny has been working for a social impact Venture Capital organization. She is based in London, UK, and she supports, advises, and coaches entrepreneurs worldwide on challenges associated with start-ups and scale-ups. Penny is also an advisor for another investment firm focused on entrepreneurs in emerging markets. She is on the board of one of Africa's fastest-growing ED Tech organizations and has also spent over 20 years helping to build organizations as well as managing the implementation side of acquisition and been involved in successful turnarounds.

Penny was one of the "original team members" who helped to build ProFlowers from ground floor to over $600 million, as well as being on the executive team that took the company through the IPO, and she continued in her capacity when the company was publicly traded.

Penny can be contacted at https://www.linkedin.com/in/pennyhandscomb.

AMY KOSTERLITZ

A my Kosterlitz is an executive coach who, for the past eight years of her four-decade professional career, has coached leaders in law, government, nonprofits, healthcare and business. Amy brings insight to coaching from her diverse professional experiences, including as lead attorney representing corporations and public agencies in complex legal matters and resolving high-profile disputes; as a senior partner with responsibility for building and managing a law firm and training and mentoring junior attorneys; as leader of multidisciplinary teams on complex land development projects; and as an expert on public task forces and a member of nonprofit boards.

Amy provides support for her clients to better align their professional lives with their values and priorities and to clarify and achieve their goals. Coaching topics often include enhancing leaders' confidence and presence; improving skills in management, communication and conflict resolution; developing a new career vision or advancement plan; finding work-life balance and coping with stress; and navigating transitions. Amy often uses stakeholder feedback as a tool for helping her clients improve self-awareness and achieve their professional development goals.

Amy consults with organizations on strategic planning, team-building, and creative problem-solving. She assists organizational clients to plan and facilitate productive meetings and retreats. Amy has published articles on a number of coaching topics, including "The Four Traits of Confidence: Growth Mindset, Courage, Grit, and Self-Compassion," featured in the American Bar Association's publication *The Woman Advocate.*

Amy is a native of the Pacific Northwest, where she obtained her BA and JD with honors from the University of Oregon. She is a Hudson Institute Master Coach and Professional Certified Coach through the International Coach Federation. She has lived and worked the past 40 years in Seattle, Washington, where she enjoys activities such as hiking, biking, skiing, and tennis. Amy is an active community volunteer, including Board leadership at the YWCA of the Seattle area. Amy loves learning about other cultures through international travel and reading. She is married, a mother of adult sons and a grandmother, and relishes spending time with her family.

You can reach her at amy@amykosterlitz.com or https://www.linkedin.com/in/amy-kosterlitz

KATHLEEN MARRON

Kathleen Marron serves as executive coach, mediator, and expert on emotional intelligence and gender diversity to help individuals, teams, and organizations align passion to purpose, to achieve results. Facilitating transformational change and measurable results, Kathleen works with business leaders, teams, and organizations of all sizes in a wide range of sectors, including law, healthcare, and finance. In particular, she has significant expertise equipping women and men to lead more effectively together with power, purpose, and presence.

Kathleen brings a wealth of professional experience to the coaching field from her two decades as a trial lawyer and equity partner in a national law firm, where she served in a number of leadership roles as rainmaker and mentor of other attorneys. She also led Bar Association diversity task forces, served in leadership on boards, and continues to speak and teach on a wide variety of topics. [Check out her ZED talk on www.marronalliance.com!] She has hands-on experience building and leading strong gender-diverse, cross-functional teams, and facilitating business growth and risk management.

As a Master Executive Coach, Kathleen has worked with individuals and teams to facilitate change, growth, and leadership development, as well as to increase gender and emotional intelligence. She also coaches leaders on advocacy and communication skills, key components of executive presence. As a former jazz musician (and actress), Kathleen firmly believes in the value of practice; she incorporates specific practices for change into her coaching.

She regularly uses stakeholder feedback to equip her clients to deepen their self-awareness and achieve results. She co-authored *Fearless Feedback* to create the guide she wished she had when she entered the coaching field.

Kathleen is a Hudson Institute Master Coach and Professional Certified Coach through ICF. She is certified in numerous coaching tools, including on emotional intelligence, leadership styles, conflict and change management, polarity management, and team development. She obtained her JD and BA *summa cum laude* from the University of Minnesota, and is a certified mediator.

Kathleen lives in Minnesota with her husband of 30 years and enjoys spending time with their extended friends and family, especially their two adult children who live and practice law nearby. She delights in the outdoors and in activities such as golfing, hiking, drawing, singing, fishing, skiing, cooking, travel, and photography.

Email her at kamarron@marronalliance.com or https://www.linkedin.com/in/kathleenamarron/

KELLY L. ROSS

Kelly is a coach, learning and talent strategist, and facilitator with global experience. Kelly's work is in leadership development and talent management—the people side of business. She works with individuals in one-on-one coaching engagements, with teams to clarify goals and increase effectiveness, and with organizations to build and implement learning and talent strategies. Kelly brings experience working in more than 25 countries, with indi-

viduals and organizations across industries and sectors, and nearly a decade of experience at McKinsey & Company.

Kelly's broad understanding of business needs, cultural differences, and the global marketplace aid her in developing great leaders and teams. Her global work experience brings an array of resources and ideas to support you on your journey.

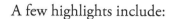

A few highlights include:

- MS Learning and Organizational Change, Northwestern University
- Coaching certification, Hudson Institute
- Master Coach certification, Hudson Institute
- Professional Certified Coach (PCC) accreditation, International Coach Federation
- Certification in several assessments, including: Myers-Briggs (MBTI) Steps I and II, Hogan Assessment System: Lead Series, Integrative Enneagram IEQ9, Leadership Circle 360 Profile, Creatrix innovation assessment, Conflict Dynamics Profile, VOICES 360, PDI Profilor 360, and Team Coaching International's Team Diagnostic

Kelly loves being outside hiking, cycling, and skiing. Travel and photography are passions of Kelly's. Ask her about the 46 countries she has visited.

Kelly L. Ross

kelly@rossassociates.com

www.rossassociates.com

https://www.linkedin.com/in/kellylross/

LORI SIEGWORTH

Lori serves as Vice President, Corporate Programs for the Hudson Institute of Coaching, and as President and CEO of Grais Partners. Lori provides best-in-class executive coaching, consulting, and advisory services to leaders who are committed to establishing compelling strategic goals, to successfully executing large-scale change and to fully realizing the highest possible performance for themselves, for their teams, and for the organizations that they serve.

A seasoned senior executive herself, Lori brings over twenty-five years of experience working in Fortune 100 and other large public companies. She has worked at the executive level for seventeen years, four of which were in international financial services serving international markets. As a proven C-Suite executive, she has broad and deep multifunctional experience in the areas of strategy, executive coaching, culture-building, change execution, human resources, organization development, brand/marketing, consumer and business sales and service, corporate communication, business process improvement, mergers/acquisitions, and board leadership.

As coach, consultant, and advisor, Lori has worked with executives, teams, and organizations across multiple functions for "household name" companies in financial services, insurance, healthcare, manufacturing, consumer products, higher education, professional services, and nonprofit industries. Lori accelerates professional breakthroughs for executives at all levels. She teams with clients to facilitate personal insights which lead to deep understanding of themselves, their strengths, and their blind spots/barriers to enable positive change.

Lori holds a Bachelor's degree *cum laude* in Communication, with a specialization in Business and a Master of Organization Development from Bowling Green University. She earned the Master Coach credential from the Hudson Institute of Coaching, where she serves on the faculty for Individual and Corporate Coaching Certification Programs. She is a Professional Certified Coach (PCC) with the International Coach Federation. Lori is accredited as a coach supervisor by the Coaching Supervision Academy, Ltd. (London, England). She is certified to administrate multiple leadership assessments.

Lori is passionate about community involvement and has served in senior board positions with United Way of Central Ohio, Franklin Park Conservatory, Project InVEST, and the Bowling Green State University Business Advisory Board. She was named by Women for Economic and Leadership Development as "One of Twelve Women You Should Know." Lori has traveled extensively across the globe and particularly enjoys visiting her family in Europe. She is based in Columbus, Ohio.

Email her at lori@graispartners.com or lori.siegworth@hudson-institute.com or visit her on LinkedIn at: www.linkedin.com/in/lorraine-lori-siegworth-mod-cmhic-dip-cs-254b8678

TIM SIGNORELLI

Using his executive background in visioning, strategic planning, and activating effective teams, Tim is accomplished in helping leaders clarify goals, so they can effectively communicate the vision and action steps and engage people throughout the organization. He is also experienced in strategic planning and board retreat facilitation.

Tim earned his coaching certification at the highly regarded Hudson Institute of Coaching in 2010. He is now a Certified Hudson Institute Coach and an Authorized Facilitator of a Team Diagnostic™ assessment tool and improvement process from Team Coaching International. He also has committed to developing self-as-coach in service of client success. He has received the designation of Hudson Master Coach from the Hudson Institute of Coaching in Santa Barbara, California. In addition, Tim is certified in the EQ in A profile from Learning in Action Technologies. He also earned PCC (Professional Certified Coach) from the International Coaching Federation. He has Master's in Health System Administration, Webster University, and Bachelor of Science in Psychology, St. Louis University.

Tim has worked and lived in Minneapolis, Minnesota, for the last 40 years. He is happily married with four adult children and two grandchildren. He especially loves fitness, golf, singing in choir, being on water, in the outdoors, and with his loving family.

Tim can be reached at Tim@Balanciasolutions.com or https://www.linkedin.com/in/timsignorelli/

Made in the USA
Lexington, KY
31 January 2019